HOPE

—— OF ——

GLORY

FILLING YOURSELF WITH THE
PROMISES OF GOD

SCOTT WHITE

HOPE OF GLORY
FILLING YOURSELF WITH THE PROMISES OF GOD

iUniverse books may be ordered through booksellers or by contacting:

iUniverse
1663 Liberty Drive
Bloomington, IN 47403
www.iuniverse.com
1-800-Authors (1-800-288-4677)

ISBN: 978-1-5320-8500-0 (sc)
ISBN: 978-1-5320-9377-7 (e)

Library of Congress Control Number: 2020904214

Print information available on the last page.

iUniverse rev. date: 03/02/2020

To the saints at the Central Oconee Church of Christ.

You've helped make me a better teacher, a better preacher, a better student of God's word, and you've helped make me a better Christian.

Contents

Hope Rises Up ix
Introduction xi

Part: 1 Fill Your Life with Faith

    Chapter 1   The Birthday Story 1
    Chapter 2   Three Forgotten Men 11
    Chapter 3   The Courage to Believe 21
    Chapter 4   See It Through 31

Part: 2 Fill Your Days with Love

    Chapter 5   I Love My Father 45
    Chapter 6   Immeasurable Love 55
    Chapter 7   Do You Really Believe You Can Give Love? 69
    Chapter 8   Giving Mercy and Forgiveness 87

Part: 3 Fill Your Heart with Hope

    Chapter 9   The Journal 109
    Chapter 10 Leah's Legacy 123
    Chapter 11 Hope 139
    Chapter 12 The Promise of Hope 153

Afterword 171
All This and Heaven Too 175
Acknowledgments 177

Hope Rises Up

Hope rises up on gentle wings of hearts' desires and wistful dreams.

She soars so high it sometimes seems just fueled by wild imaginings.

And as she flies above the clouds, above the noises of the crowd,

Hope lifts her head up strong and proud and lifts her voice up clear and loud.

There's nothing like the song that hope can sing.

Hope's song is sweet and crystal clear, and if we take the time to hear,

It calms the heart all filled with fear and guides us home when night is near.

And when it seems all strength is gone, the days too short, the nights too long,

Hope lights the pathway to the dawn and lifts us up to carry on.

There's nothing like the joy when hope appears.

We hope to live today in peace and for a bright tomorrow.

And though we know that it will come, we hope for no more sorrow.

We hope to see our dreams come true, happy endings to each story.

But when we find the peace of God, we find the hope of glory.

Hope's peace is in a newborn child, a gentle touch, a caring smile.

It's there when storms blow hard and wild, in the unseen sight of our next mile.

Hope soothes and calms, it cheers and mends. Then when we reach the journey's end,

Hope reaches out and folds us in and introduces our best friend,

The One who's been beside us all the while.

There's nothing like the hope in Jesus's smile.

Introduction

The Darkest Hour

To them God willed to make known what are the
riches of the glory of this mystery among the Gentiles:
which is Christ in you, the hope of glory.
—Colossians 1:27 (NKJV)

Hope is a waking dream.
—Aristotle

The year was 1942. Around the world, there were wars and rumors of war. Nazi aggression had overrun Europe, and Great Britain was all that stood in the way of total conquest. But any day, the fragile defense that had staved off seemingly invincible air power was threatened with collapse with each new attack. The Soviet Union had been invaded, and Germany's soldiers stood poised to finish off the Red Army.

On the other side of the world, Japan had conquered nation after nation, island after island. Manchuria, Korea, China, and French Indo-China had all fallen. The Imperial Japanese Army and Navy also seemed too great a foe to overcome. Pearl Harbor, the home of the US Pacific fleet, had suffered that crushing sneak attack on December 7, 1941. In the Philippines, American soldiers had fought a brilliant retreat, but they were finally forced to surrender.

It was probably the darkest hour in the history of this country, arguably the darkest hour in the history of the world. Against this backdrop, a minister and well-known songwriter, Robert Emmett Winsett, sat down and penned a hymn called "Jesus Is Coming Soon." The words were crafted as a way to comment on the world situation. Here are the words to the first verse and the chorus:

> Troublesome times are here filling men's hearts with fear,
> Freedom we all hold dear now is at stake;
> Humbling your hearts to God saves from the chast'ning rod.
> Seek the way pilgrims trod, Christians awake.
> Jesus is coming soon morning or night of noon
> Many will meet their doom, trumpets will sound.
> All of the dead shall rise, righteous meet in the skies
> Going where no one dies, heavenward bound.[1]

Mr. Winsett, I'm sure, wanted to find a way to bring comfort and hope to the millions who stood by, helplessly watching the advancing juggernaut of evil and tyranny. Hitler and Tojo could run roughshod over Europe and the Pacific. They could slay millions of innocent people and plunder the resources and treasuries of conquered nations, but Jesus would soon put a stop to it all by coming again. The signs were surely there; Jesus was coming to take the saints home and exact His revenge.

But He didn't come, and by 1945, that horrible war was over, and the crisis had passed.

The hymn, however, was still well liked, and its message was easily translated to a more individual outlook, offering hope and comfort to anyone in pain or despair. So, it became standard fare for songbooks around the world.

Soon another crisis came: the Korean conflict. Superpower stood poised against superpower in a test of strength and will. The world stood on the edge of eternity. "Jesus Is Coming Soon" was pulled out,

---

[1] Robert Emmett Winsett, "Jesus Is Coming Soon," in *Joys Supernal* (Dayton, TN: R.E. Winsett, 1942).

and once again the hymn was a herald of holy revenge and retribution that was on the verge of coming.

But again, the war ended, and Jesus had not come.

Then came the Suez crisis. The Berlin crisis. The Cuban missile crisis. Then came the Kennedy assassination, Vietnam, the oil embargo, the Iran hostage situation, Iran-Iraq, the Gulf War 1, 9/11, and the Iraq War. Plus, countless civil wars threatened to spill over and famines and diseases that seemed to spring from nowhere. Each crisis brought a renewal of the message written by Mr. Winsett—that Jesus would soon bring an end to sorrow and pain on earth by taking His children home. Soon, the Son of God would punish the evildoers. Many even went so far as to abandon their jobs, homes, and friends to maintain a vigil for His arrival.

Obviously, He did not come.

We have mountains of books purporting to have cracked the "mysteries of the Bible" in Ezekiel, Daniel, and Revelation. Authors have spent months, years, even decades studying to discover just what to look for in the final days. One well-known example is *The Late Great Planet Earth* by Hal Lindsey. Published in 1970, Mr. Lindsey's best-selling book (well over thirty million copies to date) looked at the increase in famines, earthquakes, and wars as proof that prophecies from those three biblical books were coming true before our very eyes. He predicted that the "great bear from the North" would swallow the tiny nation of Israel in the battle of Gog and Magog in the late 1980s. Unfortunately for this prophecy, Mr. Lindsey's great bear, the USSR, has, at least temporarily, been declawed. His suggestion—that the '80s would see the end times and the beginning of a thousand-year reign of Jesus on earth—did not come to fruition.

Quite often, followers of Christ put far too much emphasis on the end of the world, on the "fulfillment" of signs of prophecy, and on interpretation of scriptures that have been lifted from their original context to fit modern-day events. Major wars, minor wars, major earthquakes, volcanoes, tsunamis, and other disasters and even major inventions have been used as signs of the end times. As might be expected, most of those predictions come at the darkest moments of history.

But this problem of worrying about the end isn't new. Scripture tells us that many in that time were concerned with the end of the world too. According to the Gospel of Mark, Jesus Himself dealt with it when He said this: "But of that day or hour no one knows, not even the angels in Heaven, nor the Son, but the Father alone" (Mark 13:32 ASV).

Neither the angels in heaven nor Jesus know when the Second Coming will occur. Isn't it strange, then, that so many today not only speculate about it but go so far as to give dates? Ask yourself this simple question: "How can we possibly presume to know something our Lord Himself doesn't know?"

No, there's no prophecy in the Bible that gives us a definitive time for the end of the world. If there were, how could Jesus possibly come as "a thief in the night"? But we do have a clue about the end of the world, one plainly stated and easy to understand. This is not a false prophecy; it's entirely scriptural. Are you ready? Here it is:

On the day I die, the world will end.

Did you catch that? Think about it for just a moment, and you'll understand what I'm saying. "On the day I die, the world will end." It's not an egocentric viewpoint. I know that the world does not turn around me. It's simply an understanding of what was plainly stated to us in Hebrews: "And as it is appointed for man to die once, and after that comes judgment, so Christ, having been offered once to bear the sins of many, will appear a second time, not to deal with sin but to save those who are eagerly waiting for Him" (Hebrews 9:27–28 ESV).

It is a fact that unless Christ does indeed come first, we will all die physically, and after our physical deaths will come the judgment. Once our eyes are closed in death, what we have done in this lifetime will be the book of our lives. There will be no changing of the entries in that book; it will be closed for all eternity. What occurs on earth after our departures will have no bearing on our eternal home. Jesus is not coming to earth again to deal with sin; He's coming to take us home.

If we're in heaven, we won't even know what's happening on this planet. We'll be joining with the other saints and the angels to sing praises and worship our Father. Twice in Revelation, we're promised that God "shall wipe away every tear" from our eyes. There'll be no mourning, no crying, and no pain. There'll be no worrying about our loved ones back here on the earth; how could we worry about them without some tears or pain? We won't mourn those who aren't with us because we won't remember them. God won't allow that sorrow to be a part of our eternal lives.

By the same token, if we find ourselves in hell, it will be too late to change anything that we did or didn't do that sentenced us to that realm of despair and eternal sorrow. Neither will we be able to prevent others from joining us.

Look at the story of the rich man and Lazarus in Luke 16. There was Lazarus, a poor beggar, who just wanted to eat crumbs from the rich man's table. The dogs even licked his sores. Then, there was the rich man. He was clothed in purple and fine linen, eating well. He was doing just fine, thank you very much.

Then, one day they both died. Lazarus was carried by angels to Abraham's bosom. The rich man was buried.

What a contrast Jesus gives us. On the one hand, angels, God's messengers, personally escorted Lazarus to heaven. On the other hand, the rich man, whose name we are not told, simply opened his eyes again and was in torment—in hell.

He could see Lazarus, now in the lap of luxury, comforted in the haven of rest. Once so proud, the rich man now became the beggar, asking for crumbs. "Let Lazarus dip the tip of his finger in water and cool my tongue," he pleaded. But it was to no avail. Abraham reminded him (as if he needed it) that in life, he had the good, and Lazarus had the bad; now, each was enjoying his reward. The rich man was getting what he'd earned; Lazarus was enjoying the gift of mercy and grace given to him by God.

Do you think Lazarus remembered his days of begging? I doubt it. I imagine those days were blotted out. He no longer felt the pain of the sores or the hunger for crumbs. He was sitting at the King's table.

Surely, the rich man saw this and remembered the sumptuous feasts, that palatial home, and all those pleasures he would never feel again. But he'd made his choices and had made entries in his book of life. His focus had been on himself, on his life of ease. He had squandered the blessings God had given him. The rich man may not have been callous, but he certainly seemed uncaring. Or maybe he simply did what Jesus said the Pharisees had done: "neglected the weightier matters of the law: justice and mercy and faithfulness" (Matthew 23:23 NKJV). Perhaps the rich man had forgotten the two great commandments Jesus told us about in Luke 10: "Love the Lord your God will all your heart, soul, and mind," and "love your neighbor as yourself." Do you think the rich man could forget his days of plenty? Do you think he regretted not being able to enjoy the comfort and rest in Abraham's bosom?

Like the rich man, there will be no changing of our status once we die. We cannot change a thing here on earth, as the rich man learned from Abraham, when he asked that Lazarus be allowed to go back and warn his brothers of what would happen. "If they don't hear Moses and the prophets, neither will they be convinced if someone should rise from the dead," Abraham told him. So, for all intents and purposes, the day we die will be the day the world will end.

Okay, then, the world ends when we die. What about those troublesome times; what about the dark hours that haunt us? What about those times we see the world being eaten alive by tyrants; those times our families are in turmoil because of illness or financial difficulties? Don't we deserve a little comfort and peace?

Sure! And we have it. Jesus made a wonderful promise when He said, "Come unto me all who are weary and heavy laden, and I will give you rest" (Matthew 11:28 ASV).

Paul reminded us of another promise in his letter to the Corinthians: "Blessed be the God and Father of our Lord Jesus Christ, the Father of mercies and God of all comfort; who comforts us in all our affliction so that we may be able to comfort those who are in any affliction with the comfort with which we ourselves are comforted by God" (2 Corinthians 1:3–4 ASV).

Our comfort and rest don't come from the fact that Jesus is on His way back in just a few days or months; it comes from the fact that we are in the body of Christ. Christ has promised that "you will find rest for your souls" if you are in Him. Yes, we may sometimes long for His return ("come, Lord Jesus"), but while we long, wait, and hope, we need to be busy serving Him and serving others. We must let everyone know that the message of Christ is not fear of retribution; it is hope. Paul was very clear about that in Colossians 1:27—"To whom God willed to make known what are the riches of the glory of this mystery among the Gentiles; which is Christ in you, the hope of glory" (NKJV).

Splintered lives walk among us. They feel the heavy hand of time on their shoulders. They struggle with burdens far too heavy to bear. They're lonely. They're without hope. Yet we, with all the hope there is, find it so difficult to share that hope with them. Instead, we offer fearful predictions of fire and brimstone, of a battle where blood will be as high as a horse's head. We may bring some to Jesus with fear, but when the crisis has passed, how strong will their faith be?

Or we live our own lives in fear of punishment. We find it difficult to trust in the promises that the Lord, who never lies, has made. We walk on eggshells. We cover ourselves with cloaks of solemnity, trying to cross every t and dot every i. We're so afraid of the condemnation of the Lord or how others will judge us here that we can't enjoy the grace and mercy and peace of the Lord.

Or we say nothing. We know the scriptures; we know the comfort of prayer and the joy of the love of Christ. We believe that we can find rest in Him. But for some reason, we can't bring ourselves to share Him. We, who have all the hope in the world, don't want to let anyone else in on the secret.

But we must.

In the next few pages, I want to share that message with you. We'll look at words and their meanings; we'll look at some parables and well-known stories from the scriptures. We'll look at some men and women in the Bible who found hope—and some who lost it.

Hope, many times, is spoken of in the context of 1 Corinthians 13, where it shares emphasis with faith and love. "And now abide faith, hope, love, these three; but the greatest of these is love" (1 Corinthians 13:13 NKJV).

Love, Paul tells us, will outlast them all. That is true. But while

It's not often that an eight-year old is allowed to enter an adult conversation. "Yes," I answered enthusiastically.

He smiled again, patted my shoulder, and then stood and led me through the doorway into a small room.

The room was dark, except for the light that filled the doorway and two small lamps. Twelve men huddled together in a small half circle. All of them turned toward the door when we entered. Twelve pairs of eyes stared at me. I could tell that they were offended Jesus had brought a child into their midst, and I immediately pulled back in fear. But Jesus gently held me by my shoulders to steady me. I felt Him squeeze them lovingly, and when I looked up at Him, He winked and smiled again. We moved to the center of the room to stand directly in front of the twelve men. Then He spoke words that are etched in my memory as words chiseled in stone.

"You ask, 'Who is the greatest in the kingdom of heaven?'" He said. "Truly, I say to you, unless you are converted and become like children, you shall not enter the kingdom of heaven. Whoever then humbles himself as this child"—at this point, He patted my shoulders—"he is the greatest in the kingdom of heaven. And whoever receives one such child in My name receives Me."

He continued speaking, but I cannot recall everything as clearly as that. He spoke of millstones and stumbling blocks and of seeking stray sheep, but I was looking at the faces of the men in the room. Piercing eyes softened as Jesus spoke; hardened features began to smooth as the message became clearer. They all listened closely, watching intently. Only one or two ventured a quick look my way, but they no longer seemed disturbed at my presence. They too smiled—and even winked. They were a reflection of Jesus.

One man did speak. He asked about forgiveness, about how often someone should forgive another. Jesus answered with a story about a king who forgave a servant of a debt. But the servant would not forgive another who owed him, so the king sent the servant to the torturers to get what was owed him. "So will My heavenly Father also do to you if each of you does not forgive his brother from the heart," Jesus said.

All the men looked, one to another, confused at the teachings. Jesus softly led me outside and thanked me for helping Him. He placed His hand on my head and offered a blessing; then Jesus turned without another word and walked away, His friends following. I watched till they were out of sight. Then, I turned and raced home as fast as my feet could carry me.

My mother and father were amazed by my story, impressed that I had actually met Jesus. They asked me to take them to Him. I tried, but I could not find the street or the house. Father asked about Him and found that He had departed the city.

I never saw Jesus again.

It was only a short while later that my parents told me that Jesus had been betrayed by one of His followers and executed. I searched my memory, trying to determine which of those twelve men would have done such a thing. It seemed impossible to me that anyone could turn on such a kind and caring man. But the shock and sorrow faded as we prepared to make our way to Jerusalem for the day of Pentecost. It was a day that we looked forward to every year, more than just a time of deep meaning. After all, a journey to such a large and wonderful city was quite an adventure for those of us from this little town of fishermen and laborers.

Jerusalem was alive with excitement that year. Everywhere, there were still stories of Jesus. Some people were still mourning His death; some were still celebrating. There were foreigners as well. There were those who said that Jesus had returned and had been seen by His disciples and many others. These rumors were dismissed by most. But an eight-year-old believes; a child is not too wise to think that such a thing is not possible. Then, on the day itself, all the excitement and anticipation and rumors came together in one wild, fantastic event.

We were walking to the temple when suddenly we were caught up in a massive rush of people. They were all headed for a large house near the center of the district. As we flowed on with the crowd, we heard snatches of reports on what had happened. There had been the noise of a violent, rushing wind, followed by an unbelievable sight: tongues of fire had settled on the heads of men in the house. After that, these

I had been washed clean by the blood of the Lamb, to know that I was in His protection and that I had entered into His kingdom.

Now, it has been almost thirty-nine years since that day. I feel so privileged to have been able to serve my Lord for these many years. Each day of each year, I've tried to keep the heart of a child. My eyes light up when I have the opportunity to talk to people about Jesus and to teach them of His kingdom. I want to turn cartwheels when I see someone immersed to become a part of the Lord's body.

My children and my friends, I pray you have noticed this childlike attitude in me, and I pray you have understood it. Some of you, I know, think I am mad at times, but I just cannot keep the joy in my Lord from escaping.

Share that with me.

But if you find yourself losing it, look to these children and grandchildren of yours. See how wide their eyes have been at my story? They are willing to listen; they are willing to believe. Learn from their wisdom. Know that the Lord loves His children—young and old.

2

Three Forgotten Men

But without faith it is impossible to please Him, for he who comes to God must believe that He is, and that He is a rewarder of those who diligently seek Him.

—Hebrews 11:6 (NKJV)

Let him who would move the world first move himself.

—Socrates

Most people just don't like change. You may be one of those. I'm not particularly fond of it myself. But whether we like it or not, change is a part of life.

It begins the moment we're conceived. A baby grows in the womb from a tiny embryo to a big baby—sometimes a very big baby. After birth facial features change, hair color may change, and size definitely will change. Hopefully, the diapers will change too!

If you have children, you know exactly what I mean. You know how much your children have changed from year to year. There's a video on YouTube that chronicles a young lady as she grows from a baby to a twelve-year-old child. Over the course of the short video, you can see how her face fills out and how her features change; you can even see teeth disappear and new ones take their place.

But all of those are just outer changes. As you watch the video you can also see the real changes that happen. The effects of the growth of her mind and her emotions can be seen in her changing looks. Her hairstyle, the way she dresses, even the expressions on her face change in each photo.

Change is inevitable (except in vending machines!). As we grow, we change our favorite foods, our favorite sports, our favorite TV shows, and our favorite songs. We go to college and change our majors. We get out into the world and change where we live or where we work. Sometimes, this change takes place because we want it; sometimes, it takes place because we're forced into it. Sometimes, we change just for the sake of change. In the end, though, our hope is that all our changes will be for the better.

As might be expected, the Bible talks a lot about change or the lack thereof. Sometimes, the stories are big. Jonah comes to mind immediately. It took a storm and a giant fish, but he finally changed his mind and did as God asked. The same can be said for Saul, who had to be blinded by the light before he could see it. Sometimes, the stories are much smaller but no less important. People changed their vocations, changed their locations, and changed their entire belief systems based on promises, for a hope for something better. What they did took faith. But it also took some action on their part. As James said in his letter, "Thus also faith by itself, if it does not have works, is dead." If you look at the verse at the beginning of this chapter, you'll see that the writer of Hebrews also believed in the need for action. If we want to please God, we must diligently seek Him. Later, in chapter 11, he spent a considerable amount of time listing a host of people who did just that.

That chapter is commonly known as the "Hall of Fame of Faith" for its citations of those actions. Those men and women are not the only examples of faith in the Old Testament, but they are sterling examples. Unfortunately, the writer chose not to put any New Testament people in that list, though there are plenty of examples. The obvious choices for the New Testament wing of the Hall of Fame would be men like Paul, Barnabas, and Peter and women like Dorcas and Priscilla. All of these exhibited the faith to change.

But there are others, and in this chapter, I would like to nominate three men: Joseph, Onesimus, and Ananias. All three of these men exhibited the faith to change. They were all willing to change their directions, change their attitudes, and change their hearts.

Joseph

Jimmy Dean, famous country singer and seller of sausage, once said, "I can't change the direction of the wind, but I can adjust my sails to reach my destination." That's true of everyone, and one of the best examples is Joseph.

We don't read much about him, so we don't know much about him.

We know that he was a carpenter. Matthew 1:19 tells us that he was a just man. He wasn't willing to shame Mary when he found out she was pregnant. No, he would put her away quietly. But late one night, an angel came and told him that it was okay, that Mary would have a son, and that Joseph should name him Jesus. So he did as the angel told him and married Mary.

In the next chapter, Jesus is born in Bethlehem, just as the prophets had said. Soon, shepherds come to visit Joseph and his family. Then, wise men from the East come to call. But after the excitement dies down, an angel again comes to Joseph and tells him that Israel is not a safe place to raise his family. The angel instructs Joseph to take his family to Egypt. The next day, Joseph takes his wife and newborn son and moves to Egypt. Now, think about it for a moment. They were only in Bethlehem to pay their taxes; surely, they left some of their personal belongings in their hometown. I can imagine that Joseph was probably somewhat in demand as a carpenter. Yet this man had the faith to adjust his sails and change his direction on the command of an angel.

Sometime later, Herod, the man who wanted to kill Jesus, died, and the angel once again came to Joseph, telling him it was okay for them to go home. He adjusted the sails again and left for home. But he was afraid when he heard who had taken Herod's place as ruler, and an angel was sent to him *again* to lead him to another place—Nazareth. Joseph did as the angel instructed—again! All of this fulfilled Old Testament prophecies.

But there's so much to be learned in the brief story of Joseph.

Read the first two chapters of Matthew and the second chapter of Luke. Matthew 1:24 tells us, "Joseph ... did as the angel of the Lord commanded him" (NKJV). In Matthew 2:14, we read, "and he arose and took the child and his mother by night, and departed to Egypt" (NKJV). And in Matthew 2:22, we're told, "Being warned of God in a dream, he turned aside into the parts of Galilee" (NKJV).

What caused Joseph to change his mind, change his direction, buck the system, and marry a woman who seemed to have cheated on him, even before the "I do's"? Why continue to listen to angels when they give you not one, not two, but three different instructions on where to raise your family?

Faith means much more than just saying "I believe." James tells us that even the demons believe—and tremble. Faith means saying, "I was going this way; now I'll go that way." It's a willingness to change the direction of my life, to make a course adjustment. It's a willingness to buck the system of belief that I've always had, or my family has always had, or my friends have, and say, "I'm following God."

That was the type of faith that drove Joseph. He wasn't looking for a reward; he was looking for a place to raise his family and a way to please God. He had a faith that said, "God knows what He's doing, and even though the directions may seem odd, I'll trust Him."

Onesimus

It was a hot morning, but the river was cool. A small group of men and women stood on the bank, quietly talking with one another. After a moment, two of the men walked to the water's edge and then went into the river. Somewhere in midstream, they stopped and faced each other.

One man raised a hand, bowed his head, and said, "Because of your confession that you believe that Jesus is the Christ, the Son of the living God, I now baptize you in the name of the Father, the Son, and the Holy Ghost for the remission of your sins." With that, he leaned the other man back and immersed him in the waters of the river.

When he came back up from beneath the water, the man was smiling and laughing. He hugged the other man, then went ashore and hugged everyone. He came at last to a small man sitting under a tree. The man was bearded and had scars on his face, legs, and arms.

"Thank you so much, Paul," he said through tears. "I feel like a weight has been lifted from my shoulders. I feel freer than I ever have in my life."

Paul put a gentle hand on the shoulder of Onesimus. "It's the Lord who has removed the weight—the weight of sin and guilt. There is much you can do for the Lord, Onesimus."

"Tell me, and I will do it."

"First, you must go back. Go back to your master," Paul told him.

The words must have hurt him. You see, Onesimus had been a slave, but he had somehow escaped. We don't know why. Maybe he was just tired of the work, or maybe he just longed for freedom. But whatever the reason, he had risked his life to escape slavery, had been on the run, and was now surrounded by friends who cared for him and loved him. Now, here was the one who had taught him and who had helped him telling him to return and face the master he had fled. Slaves could be beaten and might even die under that beating. Surely, Paul knew this.

Yes, he did. He understood the law of the land all too well. But he also understood the law of the Lord, and he knew that it took precedence over any law that man might make. The word of Jesus was clear: "Servants, obey your masters." Onesimus would have to go back.

But he wouldn't go back empty-handed. Paul would write one of his most eloquent and compelling letters for Onesimus to take back with him to his master, Philemon. In it, Paul pleaded for the safety of Onesimus, and he pointed out that the slave was now Philemon's brother in Christ. Onesimus was now more useful than he had been before. Paul even offered to have any debt owed transferred to his account and then promised to pay.

The words must have been reassuring to Onesimus. Surely his faith was tested as he set out on the road back to Philemon. This was not a faith born of years of experience. The simple fact he was a slave leads one to believe that he was on the lower end of the spectrum, a man with very little hope or future. Escaping his slavery, even in the face of severe punishment, shows the desperation that he must have felt. He wanted hope; he wanted something to cling to as he drifted through life.

Paul had given him that hope through the words of Christ. Now that faith was being tried. Now, Onesimus, a babe in Christ, was being asked to change his attitude completely toward his master. "Go home," Paul was saying. "Do the right thing."

How hard is it to change our attitudes and do the right thing? I'm sure we can all agree that it's not that easy. If it were, those people who made all that money with "What Would Jesus Do?" bracelets wouldn't have made all that money! We have to continuously find ways to check our attitudes and look at the broader picture, instead of giving in to our selfish desires, wants, and wishes. Even Paul, Onesimus's spiritual father, had the same problem: "For I do not do the good I want, but the evil that I do not want is what I keep on doing. Now if I do what I do not want, it is no longer I who do it but sin that dwells within me" (Romans 7:19–20 ESV).

Faith takes a change of attitude, saying, "I really don't want to do this, but I know it's the right thing to do. I trust you, God, to stand with me through whatever happens." Again, Paul said it best when he wrote to the Philippian, "I can do all things through Christ who strengthens me" (Philippians 4:13 NKJV).

In the account of Onesimus, we never hear him speak. We don't know what his reaction was; we can only speculate. Two facts lead us to believe that Onesimus did indeed return to Philemon. First, the simple fact that the letter eventually ended up in the scriptures is a good indication.

Second is this passage from Colossians: "Tychicus, a beloved brother, faithful minister, and fellow servant in the Lord, will tell you all the news about me. I am sending him to you for this very purpose, that he may know your circumstances and comfort your hearts, with Onesimus, a faithful and beloved brother, who is one of you. They will make known to you all things which are happening here" (Colossians 4:7–9 NKJV).

A babe in Christ was asked to show his trust and confidence, to demonstrate his faith in the Lord, and to change his attitude. He wasn't seeking a reward for his faith; he was seeking peace. What he found was strength he never knew he had—the strength to do what the Lord asked.

Ananias

In Acts 9, beginning in verse 10, we're told about a certain disciple in the city of Damascus. He was sitting at home one day when suddenly the room was filled with a bright light, and he heard a voice that called him by name.

The disciple immediately recognized the person whose vision was before him. "I am here, Lord," he answered. Jesus instructed Ananias to rise, go to the house of a man named Judas, and ask for Saul of Tarsus.

I wonder if Ananias stood, or maybe he just sat there, stunned, for a few seconds. Whatever, his response was understandable. It was something like this: "Uh, listen, Lord, I don't want to appear presumptuous, but you do realize who this Saul of Tarsus fellow is? He's really been putting it to the Christians in Jerusalem. And rumor has it that the reason he's in Damascus is to put the chains on us saints here." The unspoken part of that statement is, "Are you really sure you want *me* to go talk to this man?"

But Jesus insisted that Ananias go because Jesus Himself had chosen Saul of Tarsus to be a vessel for His word. Saul was going to take the name of Jesus Christ to the Gentiles, to kings, and to His own people, the children of Israel. He was also going to learn to suffer for the name of Jesus.

So Ananias went on his way and found Saul. But the Saul he found was not a proud and boastful member of the Sanhedrin. Threats didn't pour forth. Instead, Ananias found a man who had not eaten or drunk for three days; a man consumed not with hate but with doubt and confusion; a man who couldn't see.

Still, there was the part of the disciple that urged caution. "Brother Saul," he began, possibly thinking a reminder of common heritage might soften any blows, "receive your sight." Brother Saul did receive his sight. From there, he told Saul of the Lord's plans for him. In Acts 22,

Paul tells the story himself and relates how Ananias said, "Why do you wait? Get up and be immersed, washing away your sins." The baptism took place; Saul was on his way.

What faith this man Ananias must have had! This was not just faith that the Lord would protect him but faith in the Lord's plans. Consider the fact that Saul had been a true terror to the Lord's church, going about threatening the disciples—and killing them. He had even held the cloaks of those who had murdered Stephen just a short time before. Now, he was blind and most likely weak from fasting. What an opportunity to take care of one of the Lord's most vociferous enemies. Surely Jesus was wrong in thinking that He could turn Saul's heart; surely two hands squeezed quickly around the throat or a quick dagger thrust in middle of the chest would do more for the cause of Christ.

But no, that's not what Jesus wanted. He said to love those who persecute you; to turn the other cheek. He said He had great plans for Saul, and He needed Ananias to set those plans in motion. Ananias, acting on faith, believed what Jesus told Him. He touched the man who was an enemy of Jesus; the man who, just three days earlier, would've locked Ananias up and thrown away the key—or worse.

In the accounts of Ananias and Saul in Acts 8 and 20, you'll find no hesitation, no excuses. Ananias arose, he healed, he taught, and he baptized.

We're rarely asked to put our necks in the noose for the Lord. We aren't commanded specifically to go teach a serial killer or the imams of Islam. Most of the time, we have the luxury of choosing those we'll teach. Still, we often make excuses; we allow our fear of failure, our distrust, our differences, and our lack of faith to keep us from ever trying.

Ananias said, "This man is your enemy, Lord, my enemy, but I'll do what you ask, no matter what happens." Maybe Saul would kill him; maybe the Lord would soften Saul's heart. He wasn't looking for a reward for his faith; he was just doing what Jesus had asked: to teach. He was just caring enough for others to help them learn about Jesus and to trust Jesus enough to let Him work in their hearts.

Isn't it funny how we tell others that they need to change their hearts and to give them over to Jesus, but sometimes we don't trust enough to change our hearts and do what the Lord asks of us?

Change is never easy, and often, it's not fun. But if we want to show our faith in God to Him and to the world, we must be willing to change.

We must be willing to change our direction, like Joseph. Who knows where the Lord might send us? Who knows who awaits us at the end of the street, at the end of the hallway, or on the other side of the world?

We must be willing to change our attitude, like Onesimus. How can we think that we only should get what we want when it may not be what's best for us or for the Lord's kingdom? Who knows but that the simple act of saying "I was wrong" might change someone else's entire outlook toward God, toward Jesus, and toward his or her eternal destination?

We must be willing to change our hearts, like Ananias. God loves everyone, warts and all. Is it so much to ask that we be willing to overlook someone's social status, someone's upbringing, someone's body odor so that we can bring him or her the message of Jesus?

Change is at the heart of our faith. It is the vehicle that carries faith into our lives. A business adviser named Price Pritchett said, "Change always comes bearing gifts." If we can allow faith to change us, what gifts can we bear to others?

3

The Courage to Believe

Be of good courage, And He shall strengthen your heart, All you who hope in the LORD.
—Psalm 31:24 (NKJV)

Courage is like love; it must have hope for nourishment.
—Napoleon Bonaparte

I heard this story many years ago. It's an old, old joke, and I have no idea who first told it.

A man named Jack was hiking in the mountains one day. As he walked along a narrow path, the ground gave way, and he slipped over the edge of a cliff. As he fell, he reached for anything, finally grabbing a branch, which stopped his fall. He looked down and saw that the bottom was a long way off, maybe five hundred feet! Jack yelled for help, hoping another hiker might pass by. "Help! Help! Is anyone up there? Help!"

Suddenly, he heard a voice. "Jack. Jack. I'm here. Can you hear me?"

"Yes, I can!" Jack called with relief. "But who are you? Where are you? How did you know it was me?"

"It's the Lord," the voice said. "I know you, and I'm always with you."

"Please help me, Lord," Jack said. "I promise to be good, to give up all those things I do wrong, and to go to church and give all my money—"

The voice interrupted him. "Let's not get carried away on the promises, Jack. First, we need to get you out of here. Do exactly as I say. Let go of the branch."

"What?" Jack cried.

"Trust me," the Lord said.

Jack took a deep breath and looked down at the bottom of the canyon. Then looked back up to the top of the cliff. "Is there anyone else up there?" he screamed.

If change is the vehicle of faith, courage is the engine that makes it go. It takes courage to change, obviously, but there's more to it than that. It also takes courage to let go of the branch. It takes courage to admit that we've been wrong or mistaken, to act on that newfound faith, and to make it come alive. But faith must be alive, just as James tells us in his letter: "Thus also faith by itself, if it does not have works, is dead. But someone will say, 'You have faith, and I have works.' Show me your faith without your works, and I will show you my faith by my works" (James 2:17–18 NKJV).

It's said that Martin Luther moved the book of James to the back of his Bible because James talked so much about works. A closer examination shows that James wasn't saying that it's our works that save us, nor was Paul telling us that it's our faith that saves us. It's God who saves us by His grace, which we access through our faith and obedience. James was telling us that having faith alone isn't enough; after all, even the demons believe—and tremble. No, faith requires action on our part.

Many times, it takes a great deal of courage to act on faith. I'll never forget the courage of a young lady in Port-au-Prince, Haiti, who attended one seminar I was a part of in the late '90s. As we taught, she listened and learned. Then, during one session, in what was, to me, a great act of courage, she stood and asked to be baptized. Several of the attendees listened closely, but many others challenged her decision on many different points. Some said she didn't need to be baptized at all. When it was learned that she had been baptized as a child, others argued she couldn't be baptized again. The arguing and discussing went back and forth for several minutes, but she stood her ground. "This is what the Lord has told me to do in His word," was her answer. So we baptized her, right then and there.

I believe that young woman exhibited her courage in three distinct ways: she showed the courage to seek out, the courage to reach out, and the courage to speak out.

In the previous chapter, I illustrated the need for change by placing three New Testament individuals in nomination for the Hall of Fame of Faith. To illustrate the way courage works with our faith, I want to put three more New Testament people on the ballot. These are a little different, though; we don't even know their names. But we know their faith and the courage that fueled it.

The Syrophoenician Woman—Seeking Out

The cities of Tyre and Sidon have both been important ports along the Mediterranean for centuries. Today, they are two of the largest cities in Lebanon; in Bible times, they were perhaps smaller but no less important. Both cities were known not only for their ports but also for the craftsmen who sold their wares and shipped them from those ports to the known world. They were located within the frontier of the tribe of Zebulon, but neither city was conquered. The Sidonians, especially, became a thorn in the side of the nation of Israel. By the time of Jesus, the population was made up of many different races and religions.

The region was located about fifty miles from the home base of Jesus, and in the Gospel narrative, we're told that Jesus went there to get away from the crowds that were clamoring to make Him king. In fact, Mark 7 plainly states that Jesus didn't want to be found, but He couldn't stay hidden. The account, starting in Mark 7:25, tells us this: "For a woman whose young daughter had an unclean spirit heard about Him, and she came and fell at His feet. The woman was a Greek, a Syrophoenician by birth, and she kept asking Him to cast the demon out of her daughter" (NKJV).

Matthew refers to her as a Canaanite. Of course, these descriptions are there to let us know one thing—she was a Gentile, not a Jew, as Jesus was. Yet she came to Him for help. She came into the house where

He was staying and fell at His feet, begging Him to heal her daughter. When He didn't answer, she kept asking. Matthew tells us that the disciples urged Him to send her away; they probably thought she was becoming a nuisance.

Jesus ignored the disciples and spoke directly to the woman. "I can't take the children's bread and throw it to the dogs," He said.

"But even the dogs eat the crumbs," she answered. It seems as if she were asking Jesus to give her something, anything.

At this point, Jesus's point was made. "Great is your faith," He told her, and her daughter was healed.

I wonder how long it took her to seek Him out. How many houses did she go to? Can you imagine the scene? Knock, knock, knock. "Yes?" "Is Jesus here?" "What? Get out of here!" Knock, knock, knock. "Is Jesus here?" "No!" Knock, knock, knock. "Is Jesus here?" "Um, well, umm …" "Wait! I see Him! Jesus, Jesus, have mercy on me!"

What courage it must have taken for her to approach this rabbi and beg Him for help. Her faith in His ability to heal her daughter was what drove her to seek Him out; her courage was what bolstered her as she asked for help.

In Harper Lee's novel, *To Kill a Mockingbird*, Atticus Finch says, "Real courage is when you know you're licked before you begin, but you begin anyway and see it through no matter what." That was the courage of the Canaanite woman.

Interestingly, it was the same courage that Jesus displayed. Jesus said, "For the Son of Man has come to seek and to save that which was lost." Seeking is a part of our mission, and that seeking takes courage. It takes courage in the face of laughter, ridicule, scorn, and abuse, not to mention apathy. I talked about the young lady in Haiti earlier, but what I didn't tell you was how she and all the others got to that seminar. Once a year, the Delmas 43B Church of Christ holds a seminar to teach the gospel to interested students. They come from all over the country for a week of intensive study in a hot auditorium with two hundred to three hundred others. Some walk, and some ride the local transportation (ancient pickup trucks jammed with people). They are searching for the truth, despite the hardships they face and despite the fact that what they learn may challenge long-held beliefs. Their courage is amazing!

"Great is your faith," Jesus said to that Canaanite woman. He might well have added, "Great is your courage."

The Sick Woman—Reaching Out

I've had a gall bladder problem since 1992. It's nothing life-threatening (so far), but it's literally been a pain in the side for a long time. I can't sleep on my right side because it starts to bother me. I can't eat certain foods because it bothers me. Sometimes I just "feel" it—not a throbbing pain but an uncomfortable feeling. Yes, I've been checked out, several times. But no doctor has ever found anything. Meanwhile, almost everyone I know has had their gall bladders removed, including my wife! It's frustrating.

There's another faith story in the Gospels featuring a woman, one very well known. There are two accounts, one in Matthew 9 and another in Luke 8. The action takes place while Jesus is on His way to see about a sick little girl. Luke sets the stage by telling us, "Now a woman, having a flow of blood for twelve years, who had spent all her livelihood on physicians and could not be healed by any, came from behind and touched the border of His garment" (Luke 8:43 NKJV).

Let's stop right there and think about that for a moment. This is a desperate woman. She'd been sick for twelve years—*twelve* years! Now, I'll admit my gall bladder problems are frustrating, but I just can't imagine what this must have been like or how she must have suffered. She had spent all her money on doctors to no avail.

You must understand that this was more than just a health issue. According to Jewish law, a woman with a flow of blood was unclean. That means that she was, for all intents and purposes, in a perpetual state of uncleanness. There were things she couldn't do and places she couldn't be because of the sickness.

Like the Canaanite woman, she had somehow heard about Jesus and what He had done for others. In Matthew 9:21, we're told that she said to herself, "If I can just touch the hem of His garment, I can be made well!" (NKJV). What faith she had in the power of Jesus. What courage she exhibited in putting that faith into action.

I've tried to imagine what it must have been like. Both accounts tell us that Jesus was in one house with His disciples, eating with tax collectors and other sinners (of course, with the exception of Jesus, everyone in the room was a sinner). Then a ruler named Jairus came to beg Him to come to see about his daughter. Somewhere outside of this house was the woman who was trying to gather all her courage to get close to Jesus. Then, her chance came. He came out of the house. The crowd was pressing in on her, but she pushed and shoved and somehow got close enough to the pathway that the people had opened up to allow Jesus to pass through. She bent low to the ground and reached out, threading her arm through the legs of others. Finally, Jesus passed by, and her hand touched the hem of His robe. Immediately, she felt the flow of blood stop!

Then, suddenly, Jesus stopped, turned around, and asked, "Who touched me?"

People nearby started saying, "Not me." The disciples were incredulous, pointing out that people were all around Him. The unspoken part of that is, "Who *didn't* touch you?"

It was time for another test of faith and courage for this woman. Luke tells us the woman came out of the crowd and threw herself on the mercy of the court. "Now when the woman saw that she was not hidden, she came trembling; and falling down before Him, she declared to Him in the presence of all the people the reason she had touched Him and how she was healed immediately" (Luke 8:47 NKJV).

"It was me!" Imagine the courage it took to not only face Jesus but to tell her story in front of all those people and to let everyone know all the gory details of the past twelve years.

This woman had suffered for a long time. Her faith drove her to Jesus. Her courage caused her to literally reach out to Him.

In many countries today, it's against the law to be a Christian. Yet despite that, there are many who are reaching out to Jesus, trying to get just a little bit of Him in their lives. These are people who have the courage to say, "I need a better way to live."

In hospitals, on sick beds all over the world, there are people who don't know Jesus but who are reaching out for comfort in their sickness or for strength as they approach the end.

Unfortunately, Jesus doesn't physically walk by these people so they can touch the hem of His garment. But the hem is there. It's represented by us—the ones clothed in Christ. We are the ones who can put them in touch with Jesus. But it's done differently than the way it happened in this account. Today, we are the ones who must have the courage to reach out.

Of course, it wasn't the hem of the garment that healed the woman; it was the power of Jesus that was showered on her through her faith. It isn't we who can heal people's hearts and show them the way to the Lord. It's Jesus, working through us. "Be of good cheer, your faith has made you well," He told the woman. Today, it's their faith and our faith, their courage and our courage.

The Thief on the Cross—Speaking Out

My final Hall of Fame of Faith candidate is a very unlikely choice, but I think you'll agree that it's a good one when you hear my case. The story begins with these words in Luke 23: "There were also two others, criminals, led with Him to be put to death. And when they had come to the place called Calvary, there they crucified Him, and the criminals, one on the right hand and the other on the left" (Luke 23:33 NKJV).

They were nameless characters who were a sideshow to the crucifixion of Jesus. We know absolutely nothing about those criminals, other than that they were thieves. They'd been caught and were paying the price. Today, it'd be a jail term. Then, it was death. The thieves just happened to have been convicted and scheduled for execution on the same day. But was this really a coincidence?

There are some who say that the thief on the cross, as we've come to know him, was feeling guilt or remorse and was driven to ask for mercy. I think, though, it's worth noting the parallel passage in Matthew: "Even the robbers who were crucified with Him reviled Him with the same thing" (Matthew 27:44 NKJV).

"Even the robbers"—plural. When they'd been lifted on their crosses, each was just like the other thief—arrogant, mean-spirited. But at some point, one had a change of heart. Maybe it was the way the people just kept going at Jesus. Maybe he realized his own end was fast approaching. Maybe it was the reaction of Jesus to all that was happening, as He said, "Father, forgive them, for they don't know what they are doing" (Luke 23:34 NKJV).

Whatever it was, somehow the thief gathered up the courage to speak. "Don't talk to Him that way," he scolded the other thief. "We're getting what we deserve. He's innocent." It must have been quite a shock for the other thief to hear that, not to mention the Roman guards and the people gathered under those crosses. What joy it must have brought Jesus to know that in these waning moments, there was someone who was willing to defend Him.

Then, somehow, the thief found the courage to ask Jesus to extend His mercy to him. Jesus complied.

I'm sure most of you have seen lists of the top ten fears people have. It's interesting to note that on almost all of them, two fears have to do with speaking out: public speaking and speaking to the opposite sex. Speaking out is difficult for a variety of reasons—fear of rejection, fear of failure, or fear that others will make fun of you for your voice or mannerisms or beliefs. Speaking out can be one of the hardest things we'll ever do. It takes a lot of courage.

Imagine the courage that it took for this condemned man to look at Jesus and ask for mercy. There must have been a spark of faith there that said, "Maybe this Man can do what they say He can do." Even though he was on his "deathbed," the thief believed in the impossible and used the precious energy that was quickly being sapped by the cross to speak; he used his last bit of courage to ask.

I think it's true that, sometimes, God may withhold blessings or even things that we need, simply because we don't ask, because we don't speak out. Sometimes we don't speak out because of our lack of faith; sometimes we don't because of our lack of courage. We sometimes say, "I'm weak; I'm not that good a person. He doesn't want to hear from me. How can I even think He wants me to talk to Him?"

But think about what David said: "Nevertheless, You heard the voice of my supplications when I cried out to You. Oh, love the LORD, all you His saints! For the LORD preserves the faithful, and fully repays the proud person. Be of good courage, and He shall strengthen your heart, all you who hope in the LORD" (Psalm 31:22–24 NKJV).

Do you think that there's a chance the thief on the cross may have known this verse? Maybe. His courage drove him to cry out for mercy. His courage also helped him to stand up for Jesus. Before asking for mercy, he chided the other prisoner for ridiculing the Lord.

That is so tough sometimes. People make fun of the Lord, use His name as a common curse word, ignore Him, and ridicule His followers. Basically, they just don't care about Jesus, about who He is or what He stands for. Would that we could all have the courage of the thief on the cross—the courage to speak up for Jesus and to defend Him in the face of those who despise Him.

By the way, notice that in all three of the examples I've used in this chapter, the people eventually had to speak to the Lord. The Syrophoenician had to tell Jesus what she wanted, then argue her case. The woman with the issue of blood, when confronted by Jesus, confessed what she had done. The thief acknowledged who Jesus was and what He could do.

Hebrews 4:16 tells us this: "Let us therefore come boldly to the throne of grace, that we may obtain mercy and find grace to help in time of need" (NKJV).

And Hebrews 13:6 tells us this: "So we may boldly say: 'The Lord is my helper; I will not fear. What can man do to me?'" (NKJV).

The courage of the thief drove him to speak out to the Lord and for the Lord.

The courage of the woman with the issue of blood drove her to reach out to the Lord.

The courage of the Canaanite woman drove her to seek out the Lord.

Faith requires the courage to believe the Lord will protect us, He will guide us, and He will keep us, no matter what.

4

See It Through

I have fought the good fight, I have finished the race, I
have kept the faith.

—2 Timothy 4:7 (NKJV)

When you step on the treadmill, make a commitment.
Do, say, 3 miles a day. And don't get off until you
finish. It doesn't matter what speed you're going. Just
don't get off.

—Tyrese Gibson

I was in high school from 1964 to 1969 (we didn't have junior high
in Dekalb County back then; high school was from eighth through
twelfth grade). That was at the height of the British Invasion and
American bands trying to be the next Beatles. A friend of mine, Gary
Coleman, talked his mom into getting him a Silvertone guitar. Another
friend, Keith Meyer, also got a guitar. I was able to buy a second-hand
guitar, from which I removed the two lower strings and tuned the others
lower to make a faux bass. One of my friends at church, Phil Baker,
played the drums. Now, there's a band!

We met a couple of times a week for a few months, practicing in the
basement garage at Phil's house. Gary became a pretty good guitarist;
Keith wasn't too bad either. Phil was a decent drummer. But the bass
man just didn't have the chops. The difference in us was that Gary,

Keith, and Phil were willing to take the time to work on their abilities when they were at home. I, on the other hand, would begin practicing, but there was always something else that came up. The other three guys really wanted to become a band and maybe play at some parties or high school dances. What I lacked was commitment.

The *Merriam-Webster* online dictionary defines commitment as follows:

- an agreement or pledge to do something in the future
- something pledged
- the state or an instance of being obligated or emotionally impelled (a *commitment* to a cause)

Looking back on that garage band, I can see that even though I longed to become a superstar with loads of hits on the charts and adoring fans in the concert halls, I just didn't have the commitment necessary to accomplish those goals. Hey, I wasn't even willing to buy a real bass! Gary, Keith, and Phil probably saw that, but to their credit, they didn't say anything. Today, I kind of wish they had.

Commitment is important in almost every aspect of our lives. Our marriage vows are a form of commitment; we make certain pledges and promises when we say those words. When we sign a contract to buy a house, we make a commitment, or a pledge, to pay for that house. If we're invited to a birthday party and RSVP in the affirmative, we're making a commitment to be there, and the hosts buy food and make arrangements based on those pledges.

I've always been a big fan of NASA and spaceflight. I can remember watching lots of rocket launches, and the countdowns always went something like this: "Five, four, three—we have commit—two, one, ignition, liftoff!" When the flight controller said "commit," the launch engineer pushed the button to fire the engines. When those engines thundered to life, there was no turning back,

Maybe the following is an even better example: if you go bungee jumping, once you jump off the platform, you are committed to the jump—you can't change your mind.

All these examples of commitment have one thing in common—they all require individuals to step out in faith.

If change is the vehicle of faith, and courage is the engine, then commitment is the fuel that powers it.

Neil Strauss said this: "Without commitment, you cannot have depth in anything, whether it's a relationship, a business, or a hobby."

Here's what the Hebrew writer says: "But without faith it is impossible to please Him, for he who comes to God must believe that He is, and that He is a rewarder of those who diligently seek Him" (Hebrews 11:6 NKJV).

That faith spoken of in Hebrews implies something more than just belief. As you look at it, you can see a slight progression in the way things happen. While we must have faith to please God, we're told that those who believe in God must continue to seek Him out. The passage implies that there is something more to faith than just belief. That something is commitment.

Jesus emphasized commitment on many occasions, none more telling than the series of events that happen in Luke 9. The entire chapter talks about commitment and faith and commitment to faith.

The chapter begins with Jesus gathering His disciples together. He gives them some specific powers, including the ability to cure diseases. Then, He sends them out to preach and to heal the sick. His instructions to them were explicit and very challenging: "And He said to them, 'Take nothing for the journey, neither staffs nor bag nor bread nor money; and do not have two tunics apiece. Whatever house you enter, stay there, and from there depart. And whoever will not receive you, when you go out of that city, shake off the very dust from your feet as a testimony against them'" (Luke 9:3–5 NKJV).

These men were being asked, maybe for the first time, to commit themselves fully to their faith in Him. What must have gone through their minds as Jesus spoke? Think about what He was telling them: "Don't take anything with you—no food, no money, not even a staff, and just one tunic." I can picture them looking at each other with wide and wondering eyes. Maybe there were a few shoulders shrugged, some sighs, and a couple of unanswered questions. There is no record of the disciples answering Jesus in any way, but it's interesting to think that Peter might have answered Jesus as he did when Jesus told him to launch out into the deep after a night of not catching any fish—"At Your word I will let down the net" (Luke 5:5 NKJV).

Have you ever been asked to launch out on faith—*really* launch out on faith? It can be a very scary feeling. I recall a trip to Haiti in 2001. I had organized a small team to conduct a Vacation Bible School for the children at Delmas 43B. As the date approached, others in the group had to drop out for various reasons. Eventually, it was just me. I was going to have to travel to Haiti alone, which I'd never done before, making my way through the immigration and customs processes, not to mention the crowds at the Port-au-Prince airport, all by myself. It was, honestly, a little scary. Supplies for the VBS were in a separate chest that I had brought. Customs in Haiti is mercurial at best, with agents setting fees depending on how much they think the market can bear. I went anyway, trusting that things would go well. "Nevertheless, at Your word, I will go down to Haiti."

The flight went without a hitch, and I passed through immigration quickly. As I stood in the baggage claim area, two uniformed men walked up to me. "Are you Scott White?" one of them asked. "Uh … yes," I replied. "We're with Delmas. Jean Robert sent us to get you," he replied. These were two Haitian policemen, members of the church, who picked up my bags and all the supplies for the VBS. Then, they took me to customs where the customs officer, recognizing the two men, waved me through without an inspection. No extra fees!

I'm sure the disciples ran into much worse than I did, and they may have anticipated much worse. But away they went.

Next, in the ninth chapter of Luke, there is a curious aside, dealing with Herod's reaction to Jesus. He was perplexed by the stories that he had heard of all the things Jesus had done and said. There were some who said that John, whom Herod had beheaded some time earlier, had come back. There were also some who said that Elijah had come back from the dead. Let's just tuck that away in the margins for a few minutes.

The passage continues with the account of the return of the twelve disciples. It's worth noting that at the beginning of the chapter, these men were referred to as "disciples," taken from the Greek word *mathētēs,* which means learner or pupil. Upon their return, Luke calls them "apostles," from the Greek word *apostolos,* which means a delegate or messenger sent forth with orders. They had progressed from simply students to apprentice teachers, if you will, which is an important point with regard to what happened next.

Jesus took the apostles aside to a deserted area outside of the town of Bethsaida, probably to talk with them some more. But, as often happened, a crowd followed them. Jesus, always full of compassion, spoke to the multitude and healed the sick. As the day wore on, the apostles recommended that Jesus send the people away so they could get food, since they were in a remote location. His answer was simple: "You give them something to eat" (Luke 9:13 NKJV).

The apostles didn't understand. "We only have five loaves and two fishes," they answered. "We'll have to go buy more food."

Based on what they had been able to accomplish on their mission trip, it appears that they were perfectly capable of feeding that multitude, both physically and spiritually. But Jesus literally took matters into His own hands, feeding the multitude with so much that twelve baskets of fragments were left over.

Later, when the crowds had gone, the apostles came to Jesus while He was praying. Jesus turned to them and asked who the crowds were saying that He was. "Some say John the Baptist; others say Elijah or one of the other prophets," they told Him. "Who do you say I am?" He asks. Peter's simple answer was, "The Christ of God" (Luke 9:18–20 NKJV).

At this point, Jesus told them that He was going to be killed, but that He would come back on the third day. Then, He once again issued a challenge to their commitment, one that echoes down through the centuries to today: "If anyone desires to come after Me, let him deny himself, and take up his cross daily, and follow Me. For whoever desires to save his life will lose it, but whoever loses his life for My sake will save it" (Luke 9:23–24 NKJV).

I don't know about you, but carrying that cross every day sounds like a lifetime commitment. We talk about how Jesus was beaten and then had to carry the cross part of the way to Calvary, but we need to remember that He carried it much farther than that. From the moment of His birth—from before His birth, really—He was committed to that day on Calvary. He knew that He would have to die on that cross, even as He spoke those words to the apostles. Each day He spiritually carried the cross; He could see it before Him and knew it was going to hurt. But He was committed to dying for me, for you, for all of us.

Eight days later, Jesus took Peter, James, and John with Him to the top of a mountain to pray. I'm sure that these three were honored to be chosen to come with Jesus. They may have also seen this as a great learning opportunity; after all, they had specifically asked Jesus for instructions on praying some time before this. But on that mountaintop, they learned a more valuable lesson.

As Jesus prayed, His face changed, and his robe turned white. Suddenly, Moses and Elijah appeared with Him, talking about their decrease and the increase of Jesus. Peter, James, and John, however, didn't see this happen because, as would happen on another occasion, they had been too tired to listen intently to Jesus's prayer and had fallen asleep. When they finally woke and saw what was happening, Peter suggested that they build three tabernacles, one each for Moses, Elijah, and Jesus. At this, a cloud overshadowed them, and a voice said, "This is My beloved Son, hear Him" (Luke 9:35 NKJV). When the cloud lifted, Moses and Elijah were gone.

Peter's commitment to the cause of Jesus had wavered in the excitement of the moment. But God had addressed that with the firm command that those two prophets had served their purpose and that it was Jesus who was to be heard now.

The next day, Jesus and the three apostles came down from the mountain. They were met by another multitude. Before Jesus could begin teaching or do anything else, a man spoke up and implored Jesus to heal his son of a demon that had possessed him. According to the man, the apostles had tried to cast out the demon but couldn't do it. This is very interesting because at the beginning of the chapter, Jesus had given them that specific power.

In the end, Jesus healed the boy. The account of this event in

Matthew includes the apostles asking Jesus why they couldn't do it. "Because you have so little faith," He told them.

Next, an argument begins among the apostles about who is the greatest, which was a somewhat understandable discussion in view of the healing incident. I can hear some of the points being made: "If you'd just listened to me, we could have done this." "I told you we should have prayed first." "No, we should have prayed the whole time"—and on and on. Finally, Jesus sat them down, brought a little child before them, and told them this: "Whoever receives this little child in My name receives Me; and whoever receives Me receives Him who sent Me. For he who is least among you all will be great" (Luke 9:48 NKJV).

Immediately after that is the account of the apostles seeing someone casting out demons in Jesus's name, followed by the story of a village that wouldn't receive Jesus. James and John, in their zeal, wanted to call down fire, as Elijah had done. Jesus turned and rebuked them, saying, "You do not know what manner of spirit you are of. For the Son of Man did not come to destroy men's lives but to save them" (Luke 9:55–56 NKJV).

It seems that the apostles weren't able to get anything right.

Finally, Jesus and the apostles went to another village.

> Now it happened as they journeyed on the road, that someone said to Him, "Lord, I will follow You wherever You go." And Jesus said to him, "Foxes have holes and birds of the air have nests, but the Son of Man has nowhere to lay His head." Then He said to another, "Follow Me." But he said, "Lord, let me first go and bury my father." Jesus said to him, "Let the dead bury their own dead, but you go and preach the kingdom of God." And another also said, "Lord, I will follow You, but let me first go and bid them farewell who are at my house." But Jesus said to him, "No one, having put his hand to the plow, and looking back, is fit for the kingdom of God." (Luke 9:57–62 NKJV)

There is a lot packed into the sixty-two verses in Luke 9, and what's there says a lot about commitment and faith. I wanted to emphasize the last six verses because of what they say about commitment. Take a look at what happens, and think about what's being said.

That first person proudly said, "I'll follow you wherever you go." But Jesus had to tell him the truth about what he could expect: "The Son of man doesn't even have a place to lay His head."

Our faith may make us uncomfortable. The discomfort may come in the reaction of family and friends to our faith, in the way that they question us or shun us for what we believe. But sometimes, the discomfort is found within. True faith challenges the heart, the mind, and the emotions. Unless we are ready to jettison what we've believed before, then faith becomes of no real value because there is no real commitment. Here's what psychologist Robert Sternberg said about commitment: "Passion is the quickest to develop, and the quickest to fade. Intimacy develops more slowly, and commitment more gradually still."

Passion can drive us to make rash decisions or even hopeful decisions. I'm sure that the one who said "I'll follow you anywhere" was sincere, but did he really have the commitment to follow through when he found out how difficult the journey would be? Difficulty can make passion fade.

The next person who was told to "Follow me" by Jesus, said, "Okay, but let me bury my father first." "Let the dead bury the dead," Jesus answered. "You go preach." There are two interesting things about that exchange.

First, why the harsh reply? On the surface, it seems uncaring to say, "Let the dead bury the dead." But then, we have to wonder what might be behind the reply of the one being told to follow. Could it be that the father wasn't dead but just old? The implication could have been, "I'll follow after I take care of my other obligations." I don't know for sure, but I do know this—when we're interested in doing something, we'll do it when we can. When we're committed, we go all out, with no excuses.

The second interesting point is that Jesus, after saying "Follow me," then said, "You go preach." The implication here is "do the work," make the time, be committed to what you say you have faith in. This is what James was talking about in James 2:18 when he said, "Show me your faith without your works, and I will show you my faith by my works" (NKJV).

The last person who was asked to follow said, "I'll follow you but let me go say goodbye to my family first." He seems to be saying, "Let me go back home to say goodbye, because this is going to be dangerous, and I'm not sure I'll be back again."

Jesus replied, "No one, having put his hand to the plow, and looking back, is fit for the kingdom of God."

A few pages back, I told you to file away the mention of Elijah. It's amazing that Elijah pops up in this chapter three times by name and here by inference. If you look back in 1 Kings 19 at the story of the calling of Elisha by Elijah, here's what you find:

> So he departed from there, and found Elisha the son of Shaphat, who was plowing with twelve yoke of oxen before him, and he was with the twelfth. Then Elijah passed by him and threw his mantle on him. And he left the oxen and ran after Elijah, and said, "Please let me kiss my father and my mother, and then I will follow you." And he said to him, "Go back again, for what have I done to you?" So Elisha turned back from him, and took a yoke of oxen and slaughtered them and boiled their flesh, using the oxen's equipment, and gave it to the people, and they ate. Then he arose and followed Elijah, and became his servant. (1 Kings 19:19–21 NKJV)

Here, Elisha is allowed to literally take his hand off the plow, go back home, have a feast, and say his goodbyes. What's the difference?

First, Elisha *knew* he was going away for good. This was, indeed, goodbye. Perhaps the one who wanted to go back home in Luke 9 wasn't quite as committed as he first thought; perhaps he was unsure of what this journey of faith meant. Was it going to be so hazardous that he might actually have to say goodbye, as Elisha did? Was he more concerned with how his household would fare after he was gone than with following Jesus? Jesus seems to be saying that because he was so concerned with earthly things, it appeared that this person would not be able to concentrate on the task at hand, and he would not have the commitment that was needed.

I've never plowed, but I've seen it done. The rows need to be kept as straight as possible to maximize the growth potential. If you're plowing, whether the animal you're using is a mule or a Deere, you have to pay attention to what you're doing to make sure you do it right. The same holds true in any secular job—you just have to concentrate on the task at hand. Remember the old axiom, "Never buy a car manufactured on a Monday or a Friday"? That warning is there because there's a tendency for some workers to look forward to the weekend on Friday or suffer the effects of the weekend on Monday. In some way, Jesus may have been reinforcing what God had said on the mountaintop: "Don't listen to the old prophets; listen to me; do as I say."

Another possibility is that in going home, the man might have been talked out of following Jesus. It's happened to many since then. Jesus knew that; He could see that person's heart and knew his passion. But He could also see those things that might get in his way.

Remember that quote from Tyrese Gibson at the beginning of this chapter? "When you step on the treadmill, make a commitment … don't get off." He might just as well have been quoting from this chapter of Luke. Back in verses 23 and 24, this is what Jesus tells us: "If anyone desires to come after Me, let him deny himself, and take up his cross daily, and follow Me. For whoever desires to save his life will lose it, but whoever loses his life for My sake will save it" (Luke 9:23–24 NKJV).

"Don't get off until you finish."

"Take up your cross daily and follow me."

It's the same difference.

Faith takes commitment. It's not an "I can't do anything else" commitment but an "I can't *not* do this" commitment. The Lord doesn't expect you to give 100 percent of your time or your money to him. What He expects is 100 percent of your heart. "Love the Lord with all your heart, with all your mind, and with all your soul ... love your neighbor as yourself." Now, that's commitment.

Commitment says:

Every day, I try to keep heading in the direction He has shown me. If I get off course, I get back on the road.

Every day, I work to change my attitude toward Him and toward others.

Every day, I try to change my heart to be more accepting, more loving, and more forgiving.

Every day, I seek Him out and seek opportunities to show Him to others.

Every day, I reach out to Him in prayer and reach out to those in need.

Every day, I speak out to Him and speak out for Him, through my words and my actions.

Every day, I am committed to being as close to Him as I can.

Filling our lives with faith takes the desire to change our lives to be in tune with the Lord. It takes courage to launch out into the deep, whether we know what's there or not. It takes the commitment to continue the journey and to see it through to the end.

PART 2

Fill Your Days with Love

— 5 —

I Love My Father

The LORD appeared to him from far away. I have loved you with an everlasting love; therefore I have continued my faithfulness to you.

—Jeremiah 31:3 (ESV)

My father gave me the greatest gift anyone could give another person, he believed in me.

—Jim Valvano

Adapted from Luke 15:11–32

I love my father.

Oh, I didn't use to love him half as much as I do now. There was a time when I thought he was the worst person on earth. Mean. Heartless. Backward. But the years have been kind to him; they've given him far greater intelligence than I ever thought he would have.

I live on a farm; I've lived here for all but a few months of my life. It's not a huge farm, but we do raise plenty of crops to sell in the marketplace. Although there have always been hired hands around to help, my father expected his children to work just as hard as any servant. After all, we would one day inherit the place; might as well get used to the hard work now.

My brother and I are the only two children. He's just two years older than me, but what a difference those two years make. He's always gotten up at the crack of dawn and worked steadily and hard in the fields or at whatever task he is given. He's rock-solid and dependable.

Me—I've always been the dreamer. I'd go to the fields. I really would try to work. But a bird would swoop down and catch a rat, and I would get caught up in the drama of nature, or people would walk by on the road, and I'd stop to watch, dreaming of the places they were going and the things they'd be doing. But here I was, stuck on this old farm, because my father drove me like a slave. Not that he beat me; far from it. We lived very well, as did all our hired hands. "A good day's wage for a good day's work," my father would always say. The servants were happy; my father was happy; my brother seemed happy; Mom was happy. I was the only miserable one, and all because my father didn't love me.

So I devised a plan. The plan was simple, really. I would go to my father and ask for—no, demand—my inheritance. I knew he was providing very well for his sons, and I knew that there was a substantial amount put away. Obviously, he would still have plenty left over from what he had set aside for Mother, so his financial welfare would be of no concern. Also, because he wasn't too old, I knew he would surely be able to make back more over the next several years.

I came up with answers to any question I thought he might ask and responses to any objections he might raise. It would be a tough fight, but this was one from which I was not about to back down; I was ready to leave, ready to break free from the bonds of this rural life.

When I felt the time was right, I went to him, full of myself and my ambitions. "Father, I don't want to wait any longer. Give me my inheritance now," I told him, with no trace of emotion.

He stared at me for a moment. The puzzled look on his face made me wonder if he had heard me. "Your inheritance?" he finally asked in a soft voice. "But that's for your future, son, for when I'm gone. Why do you want it now?"

"Because the future is now," I said. "I'm going away, Father. I'm going to go places and do things. I'm tired of this farm. I'm tired of digging and harvesting. I'm tired of dirt." I paused, choosing the right words for effect. "I'm even tired of you," I finished.

The confusion in his eyes was replaced by sadness. He thought for a long, long moment. I thought he was going to give me another of his lectures on life. Instead, he simply asked, "Are you sure?"

"More sure of this than anything I've ever been sure of in my life," I said with a sardonic laugh.

Father sighed deeply, then put a hand on my shoulder. "All right, son," he said, "if that's what you want."

"It is," I stated evenly.

He turned to leave. "I'll be back in just a while," he told me over his shoulder as he walked out of the house.

"Well," I said to myself, "that went much better than I expected!" I'd thought there would be anger, resistance, recrimination, and tears. Instead, he gave in without a fight. Perhaps he knew all along that this day would come. So I packed everything I could into two bags and sat down to wait.

As I sat at the dining table, nervously tapping my fingers against the rough wood, my brother came in. He'd been working in the barn, repairing a harness and taking care of the animals. He saw me sitting at the table, my bags next to me, and just stared at them.

"It's really none of your business," I answered, knowing the question. Then, just to rub it in, I gave him the answer anyway. "I'm leaving," I said with a wry smile, "and I'm never coming back."

He just shook his head and grunted. "I would have expected nothing less."

It was at that moment that my father came back. He was carrying two satchels. When he saw both of us, he walked over to my brother and held out the larger of the two.

"What's this?" asked my brother, holding out his hand.

"Your inheritance," my father said flatly, putting the satchel in my brother's hand. "Your brother has asked for his share now, and since you are the older, it's only right that I give both of you the shares that you are due." He turned toward me and held out the other satchel. "Your brother's is a double portion, as our law commands," he softly told me. "I'm sorry this cannot be more."

I reached out and took the satchel. When he let go, the weight surprised me. It was much heavier than I had expected. Then I opened it and grinned. The contents were much more than I had expected.

My brother seemed confused at the unexpected gift but didn't ask for any further explanation. As far as I know, he never has. He quietly poured the contents out on the table and began counting. It didn't occur to me at the time, but, like me, he never said thanks.

I stuffed the satchel into one of my bags. With a flourish, I picked up all my earthly belongings and slung them over my shoulders. Then, I turned toward the door. "Goodbye, Father," I said with a smirk. "I said my goodbyes to Mother earlier. She's gone down to the stream to wash clothes." I purposely didn't mention her reaction. No need to trouble him with that.

Before I could get out the door, my father caught me by the elbow. "Goodbye, son," he said softly. "Take care of yourself. Send word to us when you can." He hugged me as best he could, given the bags on my shoulders. Not wanting to lose grip of my bags, I didn't return the hug. Then, I turned and walked out the door, down the pathway, and out the gate—off to see the world. I had gone just a short distance down the road when I heard my name called, faintly. I turned to see my father standing at the gate, waving.

"We love you, son," he was saying. "Never forget that this is your home. It's always here for you, no matter what." He was waving in that familiar way of his, his right hand held high, as he rocked back and forth just slightly. His shoulders seemed slumped. I almost felt sorry for him. Almost.

But I shook my head and laughed. I couldn't allow sentimental feelings to pull me back into that web of the ordinary, with its endless labor and stifling rules. If I never saw that farm again, it would be too soon. So I turned back to my journey. Soon, my father's voice had faded. Then, the sight of the farm faded.

I had my freedom!

Those first days were a whirlwind. I passed through towns I had heard of from friends and from strangers I had met, and I passed through towns I never knew existed. I met fascinating people—men and women from countries hundreds of miles away who were more than willing to share their stories with me in exchange for a meal. I gladly paid the price to hear them weave their tales. Each day brought a new adventure, and I drank it all in with delight. Here was the dreamer, alive in his dream—visiting places, meeting people, tasting new foods, and enjoying the fullness and pleasures of life as never before! I had shaken the dust of the fields from my feet and at last was liberated from the drudgery of farm life. There were nights I was afraid to sleep for fear I'd find out it was all a dream and that I would wake to the crowing of a rooster and the sound of my brother driving a team out to plow.

What freedom I was enjoying! Ah, but soon, I began to see its cost.

Even though I'd had to work on the farm, it was fair to say that I had never wanted for anything. Sometimes, when everything you need is provided for you, you have no real sense of the worth of things. Yes, it's true my father tried to teach these lessons to me, but I was not interested in hearing them. To me, the cost of the food, or a new robe, or new sandals was not important. I had asked, and, usually, they had been provided.

Out in the world, however, things aren't handed to you. They have value. So although I possessed what I thought was a fortune when I walked out that farmhouse door, it became a mere pittance as the days and weeks moved on. One day, I picked up my money bag and was surprised to find it much lighter than I'd expected. I opened it and frowned. The contents were much less than I had expected. Though I tried to conserve what I had left, within just a few days, it was gone. I was broke. I was in a strange place. I was hungry. I was alone.

Fortunately, the one lesson I had learned over my years at home was the value of work. I knew that I could support myself that way and would not be reduced to begging—at least, I hoped I could. Jobs, however, were not as plentiful as I thought they would be. It took going from one business to another, going from one farm to another, for quite some time before I finally found someone willing to hire me.

"I need someone to take care of my hogs," he said. I recoiled with horror. Me, slopping hogs? My mind protested vehemently, but my stomach overruled it. So that afternoon, I found myself in a hog pen, miles away from my father, my family—and that beautiful, beautiful farm. My stomach rumbled with hunger all through the day until, finally, I looked longingly at the husks of corn that the hogs were eating. It was at that point that the dreamer and the realist met one another.

When I had finished my day's work, I sat down in the mud, and, for the first time since I was a young boy, I had a good cry. "Back home, even my father's servants have enough food to eat," I said out loud through my sobs. Maybe it was the tears, maybe it was the hunger, or maybe it was the humiliation—I don't know for sure. But whatever it was, a thought forced itself from the back of my mind to the very front. "I'll go back to the farm," I said. "I'll tell my father how bad I've been. I'll tell him that I've betrayed him and that I've hurt the family and that I've sinned against God. Then I'll ask him—no, I'll beg him for a job as a servant. Maybe he'll take pity on me. Maybe." I wiped the tears from my eyes and went out behind the barn to lie in the hay that the farmer said I could use as a bed for the night.

It wasn't easy to go to sleep that night. But this time, it wasn't from fear of missing out on something; it was from fear of being rejected. Just as I had rehearsed giving my father all those reasons for leaving, I kept rehearsing and rehearsing what I was going to say, and I hoped against hope that my father wouldn't be so angry that he would chase me away. I thought of his last words to me: "Never forget that this is your home. It's always here for you, no matter what." That seemed comforting at first, but then I would cringe as I remembered all I had said to him. I closed my eyes and shook my head in disgust when I thought of how I'd wasted the treasure he'd worked so hard to earn. Would I be slopping hogs at home too?

It wasn't the best night's sleep I'd ever had.

The next morning, I collected my wages for the previous day's work, slung my bags back over my shoulder, and began walking.

This journey wasn't as wondrous, though. The towns, so inviting and enticing just a few months earlier, were now just everyday ordinary villages. The people weren't as friendly, especially given the stench of the hog pen that still clung to me. The rations I was able to purchase, mostly old bread and other morsels, were spare and tasteless. But it didn't matter. I hurried along the road, making the best possible time I could to get home.

Then, late on the second day, the hunger pangs that were ripping into my stomach began to fade as I approached familiar territory. My pace quickened, despite my fatigue. Home was just ahead—over one hill, around one curve, down a steep incline, and then, just over the next hill.

My heart beat faster with each step. I practiced my lines again as I went. "Father, I have sinned against you and against heaven. Please let me work for you as a servant, and I'll be the best worker you've ever had."

Finally, I was at the top of the hill, and I could see the farm down in the valley. The fields stood lush and green. I could see people working in the fields. It was harvest time, and they were busy with their work. There was smoke coming from the chimney atop the house. My tired legs gained new strength, and I walked faster. It was going to be good to be home!

As I walked down the road that ran past the farm, I noticed someone standing at our gate. Suddenly, the person started running toward me. Then, I realized who it was. My father! He had his arms open wide, and he was calling my name as loudly as he could. I broke into a run, and soon, we were embracing.

"My son, my son," he cried, "you've come home! We've missed you so!"

He had never held me tighter, and I had never held him tighter. We stood that way for many minutes. Then, finally, I stepped back and began my speech. "Father, I've hurt you and our family. I've sinned against God. I'm not worthy to be your—"

But he turned toward the house, as if he hadn't heard me. "Rebecca," he called to our cook, "tell Phillip to kill our best calf. My son has come home. Tonight, we shall have a feast—no, a welcome-home party!" He turned back to me with the biggest smile I have ever seen.

I began my speech again. "Father, I have sinned—"

Again, he interrupted me. "Son, there isn't a day that's gone by that I haven't stood at the gate, looking up the road. I knew you would come back home. I prayed and prayed that God would send you back this way. And today, He has blessed us with your return." He looked at me closely, at my tattered clothing, and laughed good-heartedly. "First, though, you need a good bath and a clean set of clothes. And we'll do all that after you've seen your mother."

He put his arm around my shoulder, and we walked toward the house. All the way, he told me what had been happening on the farm, about the crops they had planted, and how big the harvest was going to be in just a few weeks. These were things that had seemed so mundane not that long ago. Now, I couldn't wait to hear everything.

I looked at him as he spoke and was awed at his appearance. When I had gone, I saw him as an old man. Now, his shoulders were back, his head was held high, and there was a spring in his step. I remembered thinking on the day I left how old he looked, how wrinkled his face had become. But now, the wrinkles had disappeared, replaced by the creases of the smile that filled his face.

Mother was in the house, along with some of our servants. Our reunion was just as joyous and tear-filled. She held me just as tightly, not wanting the moment to end. The others welcomed me home with genuine joy.

"I'm afraid you'll have to let him go for a little while," my father finally said. "As you can see—and smell—he is in need of a bath." He gently placed a rough and callused hand on each of my shoulders, looked me in the eyes, and announced, "He shall wear my best robe. This, my son, who was lost, is now home."

We walked to the river, and as I bathed, he told me more about all that had happened while I was gone. I hung on every word, every syllable. When the robe was brought from the house, he lovingly placed it on my shoulders. It was indeed his favorite; the one I know he loved to wear for special occasions. What an honor to be allowed to wear my father's best robe!

That night, we feasted as never before. Father sat me at the head of the table, allowing me to cut the fatted calf and urging me to keep the choicest parts for myself. But I passed them to others, an example my father had unknowingly set as I watched him at countless feasts over the years.

Everyone laughed and enjoyed themselves. Except for my brother.

When the call had gone out to come in from the fields, he had stubbornly stayed to finish his day's work. That was his way. When he finally came in, he heard the feast in progress. A servant told him that I was home, and he refused to come in. Father went to talk to him, but it didn't help. I guess he just couldn't find it in his heart to forgive me for what I had done or to accept the fact that I had come home.

A few days later, he confronted me while we were in the barn. "You wasted all that money on partying and women," he said with a sneer. How he knew what I had spent it on, I'll never know. "In all good conscience, how could you eat that feast or wear my father's robe? You hurt him, and you made my mother cry! You should be wallowing in shame."

If only he knew what I had wallowed in, the shame I had felt, the despair, and the hopelessness.

If only he knew the burden I had borne as I made my way back home, tail tucked between my legs. If only he knew the fear of rejection I felt and the sorrow.

If only he could feel the unbelievable joy and relief I had felt at being welcomed home, at having that burden lifted from my heart, at being allowed to be a part of the family again. Perhaps someday, he'll find a way to forgive me too, to let me be his brother again.

My father has forgiven me, though, and that's what matters. From the day of my return, we've had a whole new relationship. I have stayed close to him, learning all I can about how to farm, about how to sow, and about the harvest. I've learned the proper ways to plant and how to use the proper fertilizer to help the seed grow. He has been so patient with me in everything I do, helping me to understand, and enduring my many mistakes and stumbles with good-hearted cheer.

We also talk a lot. We talk about life in general, about the scriptures, and countless other subjects. He's never too busy to listen, and he has more wisdom than I will ever be able to obtain myself. I just hope I can glean enough to pass to my own children someday. (Was that a farming term?)

I have never mentioned anything to him about my time away. He has never once asked me about it. He has never once asked me why I felt it so necessary to leave the safety and comfort of home and squander my inheritance, which he so unselfishly gave me. He has never even brought it up. I suppose he never has because it's in the past and because it is something neither of us can ever change. Maybe it's because the experience has made me a different person and has helped me see him in a different light. Or maybe, just maybe, it's because he loves me so much.

And I love my father too.

— 6 —

Immeasurable Love

For I am persuaded that neither death nor life, nor
angels nor principalities nor powers, nor things present
nor things to come, nor height nor depth, nor any other
created thing, shall be able to separate us from the love
of God which is in Christ Jesus our Lord.

> —Romans 8:35–39 (NJKV)

I believe in the immeasurable power of love; that true
love can endure any circumstance and reach across any
distance.

> —Steve Maraboli

My wife and I have a little back-and-forth exchange we engage in
sometimes; if you're married, you may have done it too. We'll
kiss and hug, and then one of us will say, "Do you love me?" The reply
is always affirmative. Then the question comes, "How much?" The
one being asked will take a step back, spreading arms apart as much as
possible, and say, "This much."

"Is that all?" is usually the response.

Then, the hands will be stretched out a little further, as if to make
room for a little more love.

We've all done it—spread those arms wide to use as a yardstick.
Maybe we've used some other standard of measure, as Elizabeth Barrett

Browning did when she wrote, "How do I love thee? Let me count the ways. I love thee to the depth and breadth and height my soul can reach."

"I love you more than words can say."

"I love you so much it hurts."

My oldest daughter tells her children, "I love you to the moon and back."

Sometimes, we may use something material as a guideline. "See how much I love you? I bought these Barry Manilow tickets—and I'm even going to the concert with you!" (Full disclosure: I said this years ago when I bought some Manilow tickets for my wife. We went to the concert, and I thoroughly enjoyed it. In fact, I took her again a few years later!)

But it really doesn't matter which criterion you use; it all boils down to the same thing: "I love you—this much." Our love always seems to have a finite measure.

There is a beginning to our love. Remember the first time you actually knew you were in love with the one you love? For some of you, it may have been love at first sight. For others, it may have been something that took a while to develop, but eventually, you knew how you really felt. Wasn't it an amazing day, and wasn't it a wonderful feeling to know that you really loved that person and to know that you didn't want to be without him or her?

Some of you can recall when you fell out of love with someone. It might have been a high school sweetheart who went away to college, the feelings dying with the distance; or maybe it was a summer romance that seemed ablaze for a while but faded with the fall. Love ends sometimes too. As a passerby said to the Alvy Singer character in the movie *Annie Hall*, "It's never something you do; that's how people are. Love fades."

We can only spread our arms apart so far. That's how people are.

That's why it's so hard for us to understand the love of God. God's love is immeasurable; it is infinite. There is no beginning, and there is no end to God's love.

Jeremiah talked about that when he was telling the nation of Israel how much the Father loved them. "The Lord has appeared of old to me, saying: 'Yes, I have loved you with an everlasting love; therefore with lovingkindness I have drawn you'" (Jeremiah 31:3 NJKV).

Now that's something to consider—everlasting love. In 1910, a young man named Jacob Galomb, a tailor's son, whose real passion was swimming, finally reached the end of his patience with swimsuits that would constantly wear out. So being a tailor's son, he developed a new style of swimsuit that was guaranteed to last for one whole year. He called it Everlast. The swimsuits and other sports equipment that Galomb designed sold well, and a couple of years later, Jack Dempsey, boxing's heavyweight champion, asked Everlast to develop some equipment for him. Specifically, he was looking for boxing headgear that would last for more than fifteen rounds of practice. Everlast developed that helmet and branched out into gloves, boxing bags, shoes, and lots of other equipment. They were and still are well received and well respected. But despite having the name Everlast, they don't last forever. Soles wear out, leather splits and cracks, and items must eventually be replaced.

But God tells us in Jeremiah that His love lives up to the name "everlast." It was born before we were ever thought of, and it will go on regardless of the problems we have with our souls or the way our lives split and crack. He has surrounded us with His love, has wrapped His compassion around us, and has drawn us in, the way a mother pulls her child to her breast to tenderly hold him or her. And it's because, as Jesus said, He loves us.

Why does He love us? We're prone to being problematic and decidedly rebellious on many occasions, and we often reject Him and His word outright. He looks out at this world, and He sees us struggling in our lives, falling and getting up, failing and trying again. He knows what we've done, what we're doing, and what we think about doing. And He knows that, sometimes, we even stop loving Him. Yet Peter tells us that God isn't willing that anyone should perish but that all should come to salvation.

"Love fades; that's the way people are." If that's the case, why would God bother with people like us?

Because it's His nature to love; it's what He's made of and what He is, just as John tells us: "God is love." God is full of love; He's overflowing with it. It spills out of Him onto us. There's so much love that we can't even fathom how much there is.

In his letter to the Ephesians, Paul talks about the immeasurability of God's love: "that He would grant you, according to the riches of His glory, to be strengthened with might through His Spirit in the inner man, that Christ may dwell in your hearts through faith; that you, being rooted and grounded in love, may be able to comprehend with all the saints what is the width and length and depth and height—to know the love of Christ which passes knowledge; that you may be filled with all the fullness of God" (Ephesians 3:15–19 NJKV).

God grants people different talents, which can sometimes lead to frustration if we allow it. I am one of those who was not given the talent to draw very well. Oh, I have the imagination to know what's beautiful or interesting; I have the hope that I can transfer those imaginations to paper or canvas, and sometimes I actually do begin a drawing. More often than not, however, I just can't get it right. The elements are there—a lake, the trees, the sky—but my drawings are mechanical; they're flat. There's no depth to the images, which means there's no real life to them. Interestingly, when I started using Adobe Illustrator to build graphics for training pieces that I was doing as an instructional designer, I finally began to understand how to draw it a little more. Of course, I still can't do it as well without that mechanical assistance, but I'm learning.

In a way, that's what Paul is talking about in this passage. Most people have a surface understanding of God's love, something they learned from John 3:16: "For God so loved the world that He gave His only begotten Son" (NKJV). But there's more to it than that, and as His followers, His children, it's important for us to explore the dimensions of His love—the width, the length, the depth, and the height of God's love for us and for everyone in the world. Let's look at those four measurements.

The Width of God's Love

Boundaries are important in life. We all use them, and for the most part, we all try to respect them. Countries have boundaries, and within those boundaries are the things that make the country—its people, its natural resources, and its wealth. The governments of those countries try to protect the boundaries (most of the time) so that others don't take those things. In the United States, you can reduce the concept of boundaries down to states, counties, towns, and, of course, even our own property boundaries. Through the course of man's history, quite a few wars have been fought over boundaries. If you look in Numbers, Deuteronomy, and Joshua, you're going to see a lot of discussion about the boundaries between the different tribes of the nation of Israel and between Israel and the other nations. It was important to God that Israel understand not only the physical boundaries between them and those other nations but the spiritual boundaries as well.

Boundaries can also be personal; we've all heard about the "personal space" that others aren't supposed to invade. You may remember the incident in September 2000 when New York Senate candidate Rick Lazio strode across the debate stage in an attempt to get his opponent, Hillary Clinton, to sign a "No Soft Money" pledge for the election. He got a little too close, according to some, and was accused of invading Mrs. Clinton's personal space. It was one of the factors that contributed to Lazio's defeat.

Boundaries make us comfortable, and we are all too willing, at times, to put boundaries on our love. "I'll love you as long as you do this, or you do that." Oh, we may not say it, but our actions speak much louder than our words. Many years ago, I was at a congregation where it was discovered that the treasurer was embezzling funds from the collection plate. He confessed to the congregation and asked for forgiveness. It was granted, but there were some stipulations put on it—and not just restitution. He wasn't allowed to do anything public—prayers, waiting on the Lord's table, things like that—until he'd served out a probationary period that wasn't really specified. In that case, love was conditional; love had boundaries placed upon it. It made me wonder how the leaders of the congregation would have treated Peter after his denial of Jesus.

But with God, there are no boundaries. If you look closely enough, you can see the width of God's love from the very beginning. When

Adam and Eve ate the forbidden fruit, He didn't destroy them. Yes, He did punish them, but He also gave them proper clothing, instead of those crudely sewn-together fig leaves, and He laid out a plan in which He and humans could eventually be reconciled. Later, when God was angered at humankind's rampant sinfulness, He gave Noah the task of building an ark in which he, his family, and a bunch of animals could be spared. The project took over one hundred years to complete, during which time humankind had ample opportunity to repent. The Egyptians were also given ample opportunity to relent and let God's chosen people leave the land. Why, in His laws for the nation of Israel, His chosen people, God even made provision for how to treat those who were not Jewish.

Gentiles found favor with God throughout the Old Testament, and He spoke with them from time to time, just as He spoke with His chosen ones. Remember that God warned Abimelech not to take Sarah as his wife, and He certainly gave Pharaoh dreams that Joseph was able to interpret.

When Jesus walked the earth, He touched and taught everyone, He showed no concern for nationality, gender, economic state, or any of the other countless boundaries we people erect. His love is wide enough to reach out to Jew and Gentile, to male and female, and to sinner and saint. Jesus held His arms out wide and said, "I love you this much." And they're still outstretched for anyone who will come to Him.

The Length of God's Love

We've already spoken about this a little bit. As Jeremiah said, God loved you before you were created in the womb. The best analogy I can come up with for this is the way some people behave when they start thinking about having children. The thought of having a tiny life begin and then come into the couple's life as a member of the family makes some people giddy with joy. They love that child before the child is a gleam in their eyes. In the vastly underrated Disney movie *The Odd Life of Timothy Green*, a young couple is in awe at the thought of finally becoming parents. They anticipate the joy of holding the baby, of watching it grow into a young woman or man. They prepare themselves mentally and are gleeful about the prospect, only to be devastated when they learn they cannot have a child. (It all works out in the end; go rent the movie!)

Our Father is the same; He loves us before we're in the womb, while we're in the womb, and when we're born. He loves us as a baby, as a toddler, as a young child. He even loves us as teenagers! He loves us into adulthood and throughout our entire lives. He may not *like* what we do, but He loves us the entire length of time that we're on this planet and beyond.

We're never told in the scriptures, as far as I can determine, that God will stop loving someone. The destruction of Sodom and Gomorrah was put off until it was apparent that those people were beyond hope. The people of Nineveh were given an opportunity to repent, which they did. The knowledge of the immeasurable and unending love of God may, indeed, be one of the worst punishments in hell. A soul in hell will know for all eternity that God loved him during his life, but that he stubbornly refused to accept that love. She will know that God is love, but that He is also right in His judgments. That soul will know that the lake of fire was his or her choice. Remember what the thief on the cross said? "We deserve what we're getting." He knew; the other thief knew. One refused the offer of the Lord; the other opened his eyes in Paradise to see Jesus's smiling face. If the story of the rich man and Lazarus is any indication, the soul in hell will know that, just beyond his or her reach, there's a place that is filled with love—a love that can be remembered but never again felt.

I love all my children and will love them till my dying day. God loves all His children too, forever and ever and ever. He loved us in the womb and in the world. We know He will love us beyond the grave in heaven. It's possible that He will love us beyond the grave in hell, but He can also choose not to grieve.

The Depth of God's Love

Here's another old joke, and again, I don't know who first told this. Two men were walking through the woods one day, and they came across a big hole in the ground. When they looked into it, all they saw was darkness. It was deep. One man said to the other, "I wonder how deep this hole is?" He picked up a rock and tossed it in. They listened—nothing. The other man then grabbed a large stick and threw it in—nothing.

Their curiosity was piqued even more, so they looked around for something bigger to throw in, and they came across a railroad tie. Each man grabbed an end. They walked to the hole and threw it in. The men were looking down the hole when suddenly they heard a noise in the woods. They looked over and saw a goat running all over the place, zigging and zagging between trees. Then it ran right between them and dived into the hole.

"That was strange," said one of the men.

"Yeah, it was," said the other. At this point they lost interest and decided to keep walking.

A few minutes later, they ran into a farmer, and the farmer asked them if they'd seen his goat. The two men told him that they'd seen a goat that came running out of the woods and jumped into this huge hole. The farmer said, "Nope, that couldn't have been my goat. I left him tied to a railroad tie."

God's love is deep; it's deeper than any hole or pit, any canyon or trench. The Greek word Paul uses when he talks about the depth of God's love is *bathos*. The word is used by Jesus in Luke 5:4, when He tells Peter to "launch out into the *bathos* and let down your nets for a catch." He was telling Peter to go out into the deep part of the sea, where he couldn't really see the bottom or touch it with his nets. Paul was telling us just how deep God's love is; you can't see the bottom because there is none.

The love of God is not a surface love, as is ours at times. In 1985, Sally Field was nominated for and won the Academy Award for Best Actress for her role as the mother in *Places in the Heart*. This was her second Academy Award, and standing at the podium, she remarked, "The first time I didn't feel it, but this time I feel it, and I can't deny the fact that you like me, right now, you like me!" She took a good deal of ribbing for that, but we all understand what she was saying, because we all have the same insecurities she had, whether or not we want to admit it. We're always wondering how people feel about us, since it is nice to be accepted and to think that people at least like us. What she was trying to say was that she was being accepted as a serious actress. Apparently, in Hollywood, love, like beauty, is only skin-deep.

God, however, doesn't see things that way. God reaches beyond the surface to our hearts and minds. In Psalm 94:11, David says, "The Lord knows the thoughts of man, that they are futile" (NKJV).

A lot of times, we go to great lengths to keep people from figuring out what we're really thinking. We'll tend to not be entirely forthcoming in our answers to questions, preferring to be as diplomatic as possible. It's scary when someone here on earth figures out what we're thinking. I've had thoughts that I don't want anyone to know I've had. As scary as that may be, I need to understand that the Lord knows my thoughts and that He can see right through any smoke screens that I employ so that others can't see my secrets. Yet despite knowing what lurks deep in my mind, knowing what I hide from others, He still loves me. The same, of course, is true for you. He sees beyond the mask into our hearts. He knows that deep down, there is the spark of someone who can be a good servant, a trusted ally, and a strong worker in the vineyard. He loves that soul; He loves the whole person. He is willing for us to make our way to Him. He is willing to reach out a hand when we're sinking in the mire of sin and pull us out when we grasp it. He's even willing to go into the mire. That's what happened when He sent His Son here to walk this earth and see with human eyes what man could really be like.

Paul understood the depth of God's love all too well. In 1 Timothy, he told his son in the faith, "However, for this reason I obtained mercy, that in me first Jesus Christ might show all longsuffering, as a pattern to those who are going to believe on Him for everlasting life" (1 Timothy 1:16 NKJV).

Paul was a murderer and an accuser. He held the coats of the ones stoning Stephen; he hounded and chased Christians wherever he found them, dragging them before the authorities with the hope that his actions would end the spread of the doctrine of Jesus. Instead, Paul was faced with the reality of the risen Savior; instead, he experienced firsthand the depth of the love of God. The mercy he was given and the acceptance of that mercy form the pattern for each and every one of us who follows the Lord.

Let's put it another way: there are some places out there that still advertise the "bottomless cup of coffee." Before you finish one, they'll fill it up again. That's how deep God's love is. If you let Him fill your cup, He'll never let you see the bottom.

The Height of God's Love

Mount Everest stands 29,029 feet above the surface of the earth, the equivalent of about six miles. That type of height is difficult to imagine. It's roughly the same as ninety-six football fields stacked end to end. But that's not even the tallest mountain in the solar system. There's a mountain on Io, a moon that orbits Jupiter, estimated to be over ten miles high.

But as high as those mountains are, they can't reach the height of God's love.

It's interesting that there's an episode in the life of Jesus where He looked down from a lofty mountain to see His friends and expressed His love and concern for them.

The day had been long, and there were many people who clambered for Jesus's attention. He taught, He touched, and He shared His compassion for as long as He could. As the day drew on, He finally turned to the apostles and told them to strike out in a boat across the Sea of Galilee so they could prepare for His next stop, Capernaum. After they had gone, Jesus concluded His dealings with the multitudes, dismissed them, and retreated to a mountain to pray.

While the apostles were rowing on the sea, a storm arose—quite common for the Sea of Galilee, given the surrounding geography. Having experienced fishermen such as Peter, James, Andrew, and John was certainly a major plus, but imagine what it must have been like for the landlubbers in the group, those who weren't used to the sea and its sometimes-nasty ways. So they fought against the sea, hoping that they could make it to land before any damage was done or anyone was lost.

Around the fourth watch of the night, they saw a figure approaching, walking on the water. They thought it was a ghost, which only added to their woes. But it was no ghost; it was Jesus. He said to them, "It is I; be not afraid." Later, Peter asked to walk on the water to Jesus and was allowed to do so. But there are some particular aspects of this event that are easy to overlook if we're not careful.

First, the account written by Mark gives us some extremely important information. "Now when evening came, the boat was in the middle of the sea; and He was alone on the land. Then He saw them straining at rowing" (Mark. 6:47–48a NJKV).

The scripture isn't specific as to whether Jesus had come down from the mountain and was on the shore or was still on the mountain. Either way, it's apparent that He was paying attention to His apostles as they struggled with the storm. "He saw them straining at rowing." Mark doesn't say He perceived that they were struggling or that He knew that they were struggling. He says that Jesus saw what was going on. I tend to think this means He was still on the mountain, on high ground, so He could look out at the sea and watch what was going on with the apostles. Jesus was watching out for His followers from that mountaintop. From that height, He descended to the sea and walked out to the boat, which was now some three or four miles from shore.

The other aspect of the story is also easy to overlook; it's what happened after Jesus arrived. Peter walked to the Lord and ended up being rescued by Him. At that point, they both went to the boat. Upon entering the boat, "the wind ceased." Don't let that pass you by so quickly, because it's something we all need to understand.

Often, we're rocked by the storms of life and just don't understand what's going on. We feel abandoned, destitute, and hopeless. Others may be there from time to time for moral support, but there are those times when we're alone with our thoughts and alone with the pains, the fears, or the heartaches. But we are not alone. As God said to Joshua when that mighty man of God assumed the mantle of responsibility for the children of Israel (a daunting task, to say the least), "As I was with Moses, so I will be with you. I will not leave you nor forsake you" (Joshua 1:5 NKJV).

Jesus was watching His apostles, even as He was speaking with His Father. He saw that they were struggling. Now, Jesus could have easily said, "Peace, be still," and calmed the seas, as He'd done on another occasion. Instead, He walked down the mountain, across the shore, and out across three or four miles of water through a raging storm. It seems that Jesus wanted to make it crystal clear to the apostles that the love of God was far higher than any mountain.

Filled with the Fullness of God

Some of you ladies (and some men) may think this is silly, but when I'm washing dishes by hand, I'll sometimes fill bottles with some soap and water, hold my finger over the top, and shake it vigorously to clean out the inside. When that's done, I'll pour it out in the sink. Now comes the hard part—getting rid of all those soap suds. The way I do it is to hold the bottle under the faucet and run hot water into it until the water takes the place of the suds. What I don't want in the bottle is gone—dirt and suds. The bottle is full of clean water.

That's sort of how I look at what Paul said in Ephesians 3:19, when he said we should all be "filled with all the fullness of God." Whatever fills God needs to fill us as well, and God, as I said earlier, is full of love.

It's worth noting that Jesus talked a lot about being filled. "Blessed are those who hunger and thirst for righteousness, for they shall be filled," He said in the Sermon on the Mount. When completing His first miracle, turning water to wine, he said to the stewards, "Fill the water pots." We're told the stewards did as directed, filling the pots to the brim. When the Syrophoenician woman begged for her child to be healed, Jesus's first answer was, "Let the children be filled first." When Jesus told the disciples to fish, the nets and boats were filled. When He fed people, they were filled, and twelve baskets were filled full after that. God is not a God of incompleteness. He's a God of fullness.

To be filled with the fullness of God is to look at our lives in a far different way than do others. The man or woman whose heart and life are filled with God can focus on God, His Spirit, and His Son. But more important, someone filled with the fullness of God can focus on others in an entirely different way. That person can focus on others as God does, looking at them through the lens of God's love.

Gary Chapman wrote the book that became a standard reference for couples, *The Five Love Languages*. In it, he tells us how we all give and receive love in different ways, or languages, as he puts it. These are words of affirmation, acts of service, receiving gifts, quality time, and physical touch. The problem that many couples encounter is that sometimes one person will speak the wrong language to the other. For instance, my love language might be giving gifts, while my wife's might be quality time. If I try to make her happy by giving her things, she might be appreciative, but I'm not really reaching her as deeply as I could if I started spending more quality time with her. It's just the way we are as humans.

But God's love language is on an entirely different plane; in fact, He speaks all of these love languages and more. He tells us in His word about His immeasurable love, which was demonstrated on the cross and in the grace that He extends to us. We need to continuously strive to understand and accept the width, the length, the depth, and the height of God's love, and we need to continuously strive to show it to everyone with whom we come in contact.

We need to show that love because God loves them too—so much, it hurt.

7

Do You Really Believe You Can Give Love?

Hatred stirs up strife, but love covers all offenses.
—Proverbs 10:12 (NJKV)

Everything else comes down to this, nothing any higher
on the list than love.
It's all about love.
—Steven Curtis Chapman

I 've always enjoyed the *Peanuts* comic strip. Charles Schultz imbued the strips with simple humor, but he also managed to layer some deep messages between the lines.

Back when Snoopy was just Charlie Brown's dog, before he became a World War I flying ace and Olympic skater, he sometimes served to deliver the message for Schultz. In one strip, Charlie is playing fetch with Snoopy and talking with Shermy. He tosses the ball for Snoopy, who runs to fetch it. Turning to Shermy, Charlie says, "You know, it's one thing to toss a ball for a dog." They wait in the second panel, as Charlie says, "It's one thing to teach him to fetch it." In the next panel, Snoopy enters with the ball in his mouth. "And it's one thing to teach him to return it," Charlie says to Shermy. In the final panel, Snoopy is sitting in front of Charlie Brown, and Snoopy's lips are curled tightly around the ball. "But it's a whole other thing to get him to give it up," Charlie says.

I don't know if Charles Schultz meant this as a comment on dogs and their stubbornness or if he meant it to be quiet lesson. When I first read it, many years ago, it was just funny—I've had dogs who wouldn't give the ball back no matter what. But if you think about the strip and then think about what we talked about at the end of the last chapter, you'll see it may have some theological aspects to it.

It's one thing to understand that God loves us. It's one thing to comprehend the width, depth, length, and height of that love. And it's one thing to finally accept His atoning sacrifice as proof of that love. But it's a something else entirely to give that love up, to give it to others the same as God has given it to us.

I know that God loves me and not just because "the Bible tells me so." I know because I can feel it in those desperate hours of sorrow, when my faith allows me to lean on Him for strength, trust His providence, and find comfort in His words: "Lo, I am with you always, even to the end of time." I can understand it when I enjoy those tender mercies that He gives me every day—a sunrise, a hug from a grandchild, cornbread and milk, or a warm shower. Although I don't completely understand why, I can accept that He loves me so much that He sent His Son to this earth and allowed Him to die for me. I get all that.

But when it comes to transferring the immeasurable love of God into my life and onto others, I find it difficult at best. I have sometimes found it nearly impossible.

I know what Jesus said in Luke 6:27—"Love your enemies, do good to those who hate you, bless those who curse you, and pray for those who spitefully use you" (NKJV). Intellectually, I understand all those words. The praying part isn't that difficult; hey, I can lift someone's name up to heaven with the best of them. Okay, maybe I'll only do it if I hear that person is sick or hurting, but at least I'm doing it! Then, there are those other commands (and yes, they are commands), all of which involve one-on-one contact.

What does it mean to bless those who curse you? Well, it's more than an automatic "Bless you" when someone sneezes. The word Jesus used for bless is *eulogeō*. *Vines Expository Dictionary* lists the following definitions for the word: "to praise or celebrate with praises, to invoke blessings, to consecrate a thing with solemn prayers."

But do I really want to celebrate with praises the guy who bad-mouths me to my boss in an attempt to get ahead? Picture this: there's a woman who has a grudge against you, for one reason or another. You meet her in the hall or on the street. She looks at you, shakes her head, and says, "You are undoubtedly the biggest moron I've ever met, and you're ugly to boot!"

When she finishes speaking, an amazing comeback suddenly pops into your mind, the perfect combination of wit and sharpness. You really want to use that comeback because it's the cleverest you've ever formulated. Instead, you look at her and simply say, "God bless you." It's not easy, but you know it's what the Lord wants, and you know it can help defuse the situation. Usually, that type of response will have a calming effect on the situation, if nothing more than your enemy rolling her eyes and moving along. Whatever the reaction, you've more than likely averted a confrontation. It's just as Solomon said in Proverbs, "A soft answer turns away wrath." You've followed the command of Jesus, and you've blessed someone who has cursed you; you've done your part. Whether the enemy follows suit rests on his or her shoulders.

To be filled with the fullness of God, we must learn to bless when our mind cries out, "Get even," and we must practice it until it becomes second nature.

So what does it mean to do good to those who hate you? Well, let's take a look at the parallel passage in Matthew 5:41. Before telling His listeners to love, bless, do good, and pray, Jesus says this: "And whoever compels you to go one mile, go with him two" (NKJV).

When we hear that today, we think of going above and beyond the call of duty for someone. We think of being willing to put in a little extra effort, of working overtime. But for the audience hearing those words on that mountain, the message carried an entirely different meaning.

In 63 BC, the Roman general Pompey conquered Jerusalem and made Israel a client state of Rome. By the time of the Sermon on the

Mount, Rome had been ruling Israel for almost one hundred years. They had, understandably, instituted their own laws, rules, and regulations. One of these quaint regulations was the practice of "requisitioning" labor. If a Roman asked you to do something, it wasn't a request. A good example of this is when Jesus stumbled under the weight of the cross. Simon of Cyrene was requisitioned to carry it the rest of the way, and he could not have said no.

There were, however, some limits to the practice. If a Roman soldier requisitioned you to carry his armor, you only had to carry it one thousand paces—a Roman mile. Now, here was Jesus telling those who would listen, "If you're compelled to carry a load one mile, go another mile."

This must have been a shock to the audience, especially those officials already suspicious of the radical teachings of this young rabbi. Rome, her officials, and her soldiers were the enemy to most Israelites. Yet Jesus was specific in using this as an example of how a child of God reacts to his enemies. Do good to them; bless them.

It's just after this that Jesus issues what was and probably still is His most difficult challenge: "You have heard that it was said, 'You shall love your neighbor and hate your enemy.' But I say to you, love your enemies" (Matthew 5:43–44a NKJV).

Emotionally, deep down in my soul, I don't know if I can really love everyone. Like Snoopy, I hang on to love tightly, carefully parceling it out to those whom I choose, many times only with the expectation of receiving love or acceptance in return. I'm sure that I'm not the only one, however. Most human beings are the same. We are capricious, prone to changing our minds on a whim. We can say to someone one day, "I love you with all of my heart"; then, six months later, tell the same person, "I hate you with every fiber of my being." But the words of Jesus are there in red and white—"love your enemies."

In this Sermon on the Mount, this opening address in the ministry of Jesus, He is laying down the very foundation for life. He is giving us instructions on living a life for God, full of God's attributes of love, mercy, and grace. Jesus pulls no punches as He plainly states how a child of God should act, interact, and react in any life situation. As an instructional writer and designer, I can admire and appreciate how clearly and simply He lays out the whole plan. You can't read it without being convicted and challenged. You can't get around what He's saying, and you can't read it without understanding that it all comes down to love.

But Jesus isn't content to just tell us. He spends the rest of His life showing us how to do it and letting us know that, sometimes, it won't be easy. And like any good trainer, He gives us practical lessons.

Luke 7 begins with an incident that seems appropriate, especially given Jesus's message to go the extra mile. Let's take a look at the first ten verses:

> Now when He concluded all His sayings in the hearing of the people, He entered Capernaum. And a certain centurion's servant, who was dear to him, was sick and ready to die. So when he heard about Jesus, he sent elders of the Jews to Him, pleading with Him to come and heal his servant. And when they came to Jesus, they begged Him earnestly, saying that the one for whom He should do this was deserving, "for he loves our nation, and has built us a synagogue." Then Jesus went with them. And when He was already not far from the house, the centurion sent friends to Him, saying to Him, "Lord, do not trouble Yourself, for I am not worthy that You should enter under my roof. Therefore, I did not even think myself worthy to come to You. But say the word, and my servant will be healed. For I also am a man placed under authority, having soldiers under me. And I say to one, 'Go,' and he goes; and to another, 'Come,' and he comes; and to my servant, 'Do this,' and he does it." When Jesus heard these things, He marveled at him, and turned around and said to the crowd that followed Him, "I say to you, I have not found such great faith, not even in Israel!" And those who were sent,

returning to the house, found the servant well who had
been sick. (Luke 7:1–10 NKJV)

"Love your enemies," Jesus tells His followers; then He leaves them and enters Capernaum. Immediately, those words are tested as a Roman centurion begs for a favor, the healing of a servant. The centurion sends some friends he has made, Jewish elders, who are very persuasive. "He's a good man. He loves our nation; he has built us a synagogue," they tell Jesus.

These are wonderful traits that the centurion has exhibited. Of course, the cynic would say, "He probably just did all that to placate the locals. Spend a little money to build a synagogue, and keep the peace." Notice, by the way, they say, "for he loves our nation." There's nothing in that statement about believing in God.

So Jesus has a decision to make—to go or not to go and to heal or not to heal. Of course, He goes; how could He not go? He leaves whatever path He was on, puts aside whatever task He had planned, and goes to the centurion's house. Jesus walks the extra mile to heal a beloved servant and to heal another man's burdened heart.

Jesus did not have to go, but He did anyway. In this leaving, there are a couple of interesting points to consider:

First, on top of the fact that Jesus is love, just as God is love, He was following sound advice: "If your enemy is hungry, give him bread to eat; and if he is thirsty, give him water to drink; for so you will heap coals of fire on his head, and the LORD will reward you" (Proverbs 25:21–22 NJKV).

When I was a teenager back in the '60s, I went to good old Camp Inagehi in Douglasville, Georgia, for a week of Bible study, fellowship, and fear of snakes. Joyce, a young lady I was kind of dating at the time ("kind of" because I couldn't drive yet), told me a story of how, on the last night of camp, one cabin full of girls decided to play a prank on the girls of another cabin. They waited until the others were all gone to some activity; then they proceeded to do a number on the cabin. I'm not sure exactly what happened, but it may have involved toilet paper. Anyway, the girls went back to their cabin to wait for the cries of despair.

Instead, there was silence. The tension grew; no one from the other cabin said a word the whole evening. But after lights-out, the sound of angelic voices came flowing from the girls in the offended cabin with the words to that well-known Horatio Palmer hymn, "Angry words, oh let them never from the tongue unbridled slip ..."

You can bet those girls who had planned the prank were expecting an entirely different reaction and were prepared for revenge. What they got, however, was a lesson that stayed with them for many years. What they learned was what Andy Taylor once told Barney Fife: "You don't fight fire with fire; you fight fire with a hose." Getting even isn't always as fun as it seems, and it can sometimes get out of control. (I know, because the boys' side was involved in an escalating war of pranks at the same time.)

Charlotte Bronte put it this way: "Something of vengeance I had tasted for the first time; as aromatic wine it seemed, on swallowing, warm and racy: its after-flavor, metallic and corroding, gave me a sensation as if I had been poisoned." Revenge is not a dish best served cold; it is a dish best not served at all.

When Solomon said that giving bread and drink to your enemy would heap coals of fire on his head, it was very wise advice. Touching your enemy with the love of God fulfills His desire for your life and causes the enemy to see an entirely different side of you. It may be the impetus to heal a rift or at least create dialogue where once there was none.

Jesus, in going to the home of the centurion, was showing a willingness to reach out to someone whom many considered a mortal enemy. He was showing compassion, care, concern, and love and was showing His brothers and sisters—the entire world, really—how to handle these types of situations. By the way, this is opinion, not Bible, but I believe He would have gone whether the centurion had built a synagogue or not.

Second, Jesus was following His own command—"Love your enemies, do good to those who hate you"—and He was demonstrating how to do it.

This brings us back to our original question: "Do I really believe

I can love?" How do I take that immeasurable love of God, that love He so freely and generously poured into my life and my soul, and let it spill out of me into the lives of not just my loved ones and my friends but my enemies? I want to do it. I want to obey the Lord's command, but it's so difficult.

A father once came to Jesus seeking healing for his son, who had a troubling spirit. When Jesus said it could be done if he believed, the father cried, "Lord, I believe; help my unbelief!" (Mark 9:24 NKJV).

I don't know about you, but this is something I've struggled with my entire life. When I'm wronged, I take it personally. When someone wrongs one of my loved ones, I take it personally. I've been known to work up a pretty good case of umbrage at the drop of a hat. On occasion, I've sought some type of revenge. Other times, I sought to take what I considered the high road, which involved not speaking with that person to show my disdain or, worse, intermittently reminding the person of the wrong at just the right moment for maximum effect. In those instances, I was attempting to heap coals upon their heads in all the wrong ways for all the wrong reasons. My spiritual blinders were on, and instead of seeing the example of Christ, as exemplified in the incident with the centurion, I decided to go my own way. I might say "I love you" to the enemy, but there was nothing behind it; my words had become as "sounding brass or a clanging cymbal."

In those times, I've had to look hard at my motives. The incidents required a good deal of repentance and an immense change of heart, along with the swallowing of pride. If only I had done all the thinking beforehand.

Do you find yourself in this quandary from time to time? Is there someone right now whom you consider an enemy for one reason or another? Do you want to change? Do you want to learn how to go the extra mile, as Jesus commands? Most of us do want to change; most of us really do want to learn how to love like Jesus.

Well, I have something that might help a little, a practical exercise to help us look at our enemies and begin to understand who they are, why they're our enemies, and how we can change our hearts. Let's face it; the gap will never be bridged until we do change our own hearts. It will never be bridged until we make the effort to let the enemy know we're ready to repair whatever is broken in an existing or potential relationship.

This involves some writing and some thinking. Some of it may seem strange, but the exercise is designed to help us reduce the battle lines down to manageable chunks for our own lives. I've provided a chart on the next few pages to help with the thought process. The questions are on the left side; the enemies will be across the top.

Let's begin by identifying the enemy. We'll just do three, so it should be fairly easy, right?

Who is my enemy?			

First, we need to define the enemy. A lawyer once came to Jesus and asked, "Who is my neighbor?" For this, we want to ask, "Who is my enemy?"

An enemy is someone who is against me, those I care for, or my interests. It may be someone I don't like for some reason or someone I may even detest. So let's put some enemies in the chart. We'll start with someone universal:

Who is my enemy?	Satan		

Identifying the first enemy may seem a little elemental, but bear with me because there's a purpose here.

We all know Satan is our enemy. In 1 Peter 5:8, the apostle tells us, "Be sober, be vigilant; because your adversary the devil walks about like a roaring lion, seeking whom he may devour" (NKJV). He is looking to eat us alive at any opportunity.

Now, let's get away from someone universal and hone in the exercise a little by adding another enemy, although this may still seem a bit wide-ranging:

Who is my enemy?	Satan	Terrorists	

I suppose there would be no argument from anyone about this second enemy. Terrorists too are plotting how they can destroy us or disrupt our lives in some way. Someone about to detonate a bomb strapped to his or her torso is not a friend.

Okay, so we have some broad-based enemies to think about. But now, let's make it personal. Name someone who's your enemy, someone who's against you or your interests.

Who is my enemy?	Satan	Terrorists	

I'm going to add a little wrinkle to this last enemy. Does this person know he or she is your enemy? Put *yes* or *no* next to the name. It's important.

Now, let's ask the second question: Why do I say this person is my enemy?

Who is my enemy?	Satan		
Why is this person my enemy?	He hates God and wants to keep me from Him.		

With Satan, the answer is simple: he hates God. No, Satan isn't my enemy because he hates me. Let's be honest; Satan doesn't really care about me, personally. His main goal is to thwart God at every opportunity, so he'll pursue me to the ends of the earth to tempt me in any number of ways. But it's not because he wants me in hell with him; it's because he doesn't want me in heaven with God.

Who is my enemy?	Satan	Terrorists	
Why is this person my enemy?	He hates God and wants to keep me from Him.	They hate our way of life.	

Terrorists have a somewhat similar motivation. Whether religious or political, terrorists believe those who do not follow their beliefs must be punished or forcibly made to change. They hate our way of life or our belief system. In some instances, they hate God as well and hate those who follow Him.

So now, what do we put in that third column?

Who is my enemy?	Satan	Terrorists	
Why is this person my enemy?	He hates God and wants to keep me from Him.	They hate our way of life.	

This person may have wronged you or someone you love, or he or she may have upset you in some way. What is it that separated you from that person? Be honest about the reason; this is between you, that person, and God.

I'll give you an example. Many years ago, when I was in radio, Ralph, one of the salesmen at the station where I worked, got on my wrong side. I'm sorry if this offends salespeople, but sometimes they can be pests. Ralph apparently had been a pest way too often. Whatever it was that set me off, I got so mad that I refused to even speak to him—and no, I wasn't twelve at the time; I was an adult, at least chronologically.

Ralph would bring work in and give me verbal instructions. I would listen; then I would take the work and turn back to whatever I was doing. Ralph had become my adversary, my nemesis.

Which leads us to the final question: how do I love my enemy?

Who is my enemy?	Satan	Terrorists	
Why is this person my enemy?	He hates God and wants to keep me from Him.	They hate our way of life.	
How do I love this person?	I can't. Resist or flee!		

In the Satan column, I've entered "I can't" because there's nothing I can do to convince Satan to love me. Even if he says he loves me, I can't believe him, since he's the father of lies. There is nothing I can do for him; he's a lost cause. What I need to do is take one of two paths. Depending on the situation and my spiritual strength, I either follow the advice of James to "resist the devil and he will flee from you," or I can follow the advice of many others and flee from the face of temptation. Either way, I need to keep Satan from dragging me away from God.

Who is my enemy?	Satan	Terrorists	
Why is this person my enemy?	He hates God and wants to keep me from Him.	They hate our way of life.	
How do I love this person?	I can't. Resist or flee!	Pray for them.	

Ah, but with terrorists, I can take a different approach. Confrontation may not be best in this situation; instead, I need to use one of God's other great tools—prayer. I can pray for them and not just when I'm confronted with a situation. I can pray for them now. Who knows if God might move in the heart of one or two or any number to soften them, to convince them to be more open to discussion or to be less hateful? If I am ever in contact with one of these terrorists, regardless of the circumstance, I should take the opportunity afforded me to speak with him or her about my faith and to let that person know that God loves everyone. Taking this type of stand may mean more than just losing a friend; it may mean my life. I would pray also for the courage to take that stand. This approach may not mean anything to the terrorist in the end, but at least I will have done my part to reach out to the enemy, to go the extra mile.

Now we've made it to that personal enemy you named earlier.

Who is my enemy?	Satan	Terrorists	
Why is this person my enemy?	He hates God and wants to keep me from Him.	They hate our way of life.	
How do I love this person?	I can't. Resist or flee!	Pray for them.	

I came at the discussion in this manner because I wanted us to think about that word *enemy* much more closely than we usually do. When you think about these three that we've identified, do a little exercise. Get a mental picture of each one; then place the picture of Satan and the terrorists standing side by side. Oh, yes, those are enemies. Now, place the picture of the enemy you identified next to those other two. Is that person really an enemy?

As you think about that face, put aside your animosity, arrogance, hurt feelings, pride, or prejudice—whatever it is that makes that person your enemy. Just see the face. When you strip all that away, you can see this is a flesh-and-blood human being, one possessing an eternal soul. Your enemy really is a person that God loves, through His immeasurable love. God sent His Son for your enemy. Jesus allowed Himself to be nailed on the cross for your enemy. He commands us, "Love your enemies."

Oh, and guess what—He sent His Son for those terrorists too. They are flesh-and-blood human beings, misguided though they may be by rage or hatred; and because they are human beings, God requires us to pray for them as much as anyone else. Maybe more. "Pray for them which despitefully use you, and persecute you," Jesus told us in Matthew 5:44 (NKJV). It isn't easy—nothing good ever is—but who knows? Because of your prayer, God may touch that person's heart enough to change it.

The men and women who heard those words from Jesus had the same problem we have with the command. They had to think it through too.

"Listen, Jesus, we're talking about the Romans here. They're the conquerors," one might have said. (Were the Romans to the Jews what terrorists are to us today?)

"Then help Me conquer their hearts," Jesus might have answered.

The extra mile that Jesus went to visit the Roman centurion was a real-life example of how all that enemy stuff means nothing when someone needs the Lord. The lesson, I'm sure, was confusing to some but inspiring to others.

It was only a few years later that one of His apostles, Peter, went the extra mile for his own centurion. The story is in Acts 10. Cornelius was the centurion's name. He was a devout man, according to the passage, one who gave to the poor and who prayed to God as best he could. One day, an angel told Cornelius his prayers were being answered. "Send for a man named Peter," the angel said, and he did.

The next day, in the city of Joppa, Peter was praying too. But it was moving on toward noon, and Peter was hungry, so hungry that he fell into a trance. That's when he had the vision about the sheet being let down from heaven with all types of animals. "Kill and eat," a voice said.

"I can't eat anything common or unclean," Peter answered.

The voice said, "What God has cleansed, you must not call common." Either Peter was very tired and hungry or he was a bit slow because the scene was repeated two more times (Acts 10:13–16 NKJV).

Peter was contemplating what had happened when the men sent by Cornelius knocked at the door. The Spirit told Peter to go with the men, which was an order He did not have to give Peter two more times.

Peter went with them to the house of Cornelius. He taught them. He baptized them. His comment to Cornelius was, "In truth, I perceive that God shows no partiality. But in every nation whoever fears Him and works righteousness is accepted by Him" (Acts 10:34–35 NKJV). Peter had learned to put his pride and prejudice aside in the name of the Lord and for the cause of the Lord. He had learned to love someone who, to him, might not have been loveable, a Roman whom God had already touched with His immeasurable love and with whom Peter needed to share his own love.

Our turning points may not be so dramatic, but they are no less important. Remember my story about Ralph? I continued giving him the silent treatment for several weeks, and it would have continued forever, had that still small voice of the Spirit not whispered in my ear, "Isn't this a little silly?" It was, indeed, silly. So one day, as we passed in the hall, I swallowed my pride and asked him to step into an empty office, where I apologized for my actions. The apology was accepted, and we had a good relationship for the rest of the time I was at the station. That was one of the many extra-mile journeys I've had to take in my life.

Now, your situation with an enemy may not be so trivial. The enemy may be a father who abused you; a drunk driver who took the life of your spouse; the woman at work who was promoted over you, despite having less experience than you; the thief who broke into your house and then stole your belongings and destroyed all your family photos; or any one of thousands of other people and situations. You may have read all this and said, "Scott, it's just so difficult." Yeah, I know it is. I'm right there with you.

If you're having a tough time loving that enemy you listed on the chart earlier, let me give you something to think about concerning Jesus's command: He didn't say that we have to become best of friends with our enemies; He just told us to love them. Some of us may have spouses, parents, siblings, or children with whom we're not too happy all the time, but we still love them and will defend them against any attack from anyone else. That's what Jesus says—just love them. You don't have to agree with them or like them or what they're doing. But you do have to love them.

Now, when you make the conscious decision to love someone, you'll find the hard edges will begin to soften; you'll begin to think differently about that person. You may even see things from his or her point of view, which can be quite jarring at times.

Once, some men brought a woman to Jesus. She had been caught in the very act of adultery, and they demanded to know what should be done with her. "We should stone her. What do you say?" Of course, this was just a trap, a way of getting Jesus in trouble with the Jewish officials or the Roman officials; either would do for their purposes.

But Jesus didn't immediately answer. He just stooped down and wrote on the ground. A great many scholars and nonscholars have speculated on what He wrote. Marshall Keeble, a mid-twentieth-century preacher, said, "I don't think He wrote anything. I just think He was giving those rascals time to sweat."

After a short period, Jesus simply told the crowd that the one who had no sin should cast the first stone. Now, Jesus could have given them a long discourse or taught them some deep lessons from Old Testament prophets or, more appropriately, directly from God. But instead, He challenged them to think about what they were doing. According to the account, the accusers had had enough. They slipped away, one by one, beginning with the oldest. As I heard another preacher once say, the older ones were cut to the heart immediately, realizing their own folly. It took the younger ones a little longer as they searched for a way out of their conundrum.

Sometimes, our enemies need to think about what they're doing as much as we do. Our soft answer can cause the enemy to notice a difference in us, one that may cause him or her to reflect on the situation a little more. You may help the enemy begin to think about things differently too.

You're not going to turn an enemy into a friend overnight; it's going to take time. You may never be able to turn him or her into a friend at all. But the only way to make it happen is to start loving your enemy.

Remember what Paul told the Philippians? "I can do all things through Christ who strengthens me." We use that scripture a lot during times of turmoil, strife, disease, heartache, and many other life events. It's a comforting thought to know that I can get through it all because Jesus is with me, God is with me, His rod and His staff comfort me. He prepares a table for me in the presence of ... uh ... my enemies.

Our hearts say, "I can't love that person. Don't you know what he or she did to me?" Our Savior says, "Yes, you can. Don't love that person with *your* love; love them with *My* love!"

The love of God is immeasurable, spilling into our lives in ways we can't imagine. We need to believe we can stop being like Snoopy, to believe we can give that love to others. We need to overwhelm them with His love. We need to believe God can work with us to change our hearts and to believe He can work through us to change someone else's heart. The more you do it, the easier it gets. One day, you'll wake up and realize you have no enemies.

When you love your enemies, it leads you to extend not just God's love to them but His grace and mercy as well.

8

Giving Mercy and Forgiveness

And if [your brother] sins against you seven times in a day, and seven times in a day returns to you, saying, 'I repent,' you shall forgive him."

—Luke 17:4 (NJKV)

I pray that you all put your shoes way under the bed at night so that you gotta get on your knees in the morning to find them. And while you're down there thank God for grace and mercy and understanding. We all fall short of the glory, we all got plenty.

—Denzel Washington

When I think of the immeasurable love of God, what comes to mind is those fountains you sometimes see, where the waterspout pours into a small receptacle which, when it's full, spills into a larger one. That one too spills into a larger one, until the water finally pours into the main fountain. Then the water is pumped back up to the spout to pour out again.

If we're following the command of Jesus—"Love others as I have loved you"—this is a great picture of how our love should be flowing. We are filled so full of His love that it just spills out to those with whom we come in contact, friend or foe. Hopefully, they become filled and spill that love to others. Eventually, though, it all flows back up to the Father, from whom it first came. Love should just keep recycling.

The passage we looked at in the last chapter, Luke 6:27, and following is jammed with wonderful precepts for us to follow—love your enemies, turn the other cheek, bless those who curse you, do good to your enemies, lend without expecting anything in return, and others. "If you do these things," Jesus said, "you will be sons of the Most High. For He is kind to the unthankful and evil." Now, that sounds truly satisfying. If we love our enemies, God will be pleased. But Jesus wasn't finished with His discourse. He added a few more wrinkles: "Therefore be merciful, just as your Father also is merciful. Judge not, and you shall not be judged. Condemn not, and you shall not be condemned. Forgive, and you will be forgiven" (Luke 6:36–37 NKJV).

I've always thought one of the biggest words in the English language is *if*, because it's used so many times in statements of regret. It has come to symbolize lost opportunities in many people's lives. "If only I had tried harder"; "If only I had listened to her"; "If only I'd listened to my dad's advice"; and on and on. *If* can change your life, many times for the worse. Well, Jesus uses another big word in this passage—*therefore*. This is a word that can also change your life; in this case, it can change it for the better.

The word *therefore* is a conjunctive adverb, which joins two clauses or phrases together. *Therefore* shows cause and effect; it is a signal to look at the words in the phrase before the *therefore* as the cause of what follows it. The Greek word used here is *oun*, which means "then," "therefore," "accordingly," "consequently," or "these things being so."

Now, think about what Jesus said just before this *therefore*—"For He is kind to the unthankful and evil." Just who are those people? Well, if we're honest, we can include ourselves in that group because we often demonstrate those qualities. Despite this, God will make us His sons and daughters, if we "do these things." What things? Love our enemies, bless our cursers, and do good to the spiteful users. We take in God's immeasurable love and pour it out to others, just like those fountains. When we do that, we obtain the mercy of God, and we are sons and daughters of the Most High.

"Consequently," "these things being so," "accordingly," or "therefore," there are other attributes of God to take on in our lives. Let's look at the two Jesus features most prominently in this passage.

The first is to be merciful, just as God Himself is merciful.

When I think of being merciful, I think of it more along the lines of not punishing someone who deserves to be punished.

Back in the early 2000s, I was working at a building in an industrial park. It was nice because I didn't have to get on the expressway to get there, although there was still traffic at certain intersections. One particular intersection, Covington Highway and Evans Mill Road, was always backed up on the Covington Highway side. Traffic engineers had provided a middle lane for turns, but the break in the solid yellow line was way too close to the intersection; in the afternoons, traffic was usually backed up so cars on Covington Highway would often have to wait two or even three lights. Usually, I waited patiently to get to that break in the solid line. One day, however, I was in a hurry. No one was in the turn lane, others had gotten in early (as they did every day while I waited my turn), and finally, I decided to do the same—and drove past a police car. He pulled in behind me, hit the blue lights, and pulled me over after I'd made the turn.

I whipped out my license immediately, knowing I was guilty. He ran a check on me and saw I had no tickets (okay, a couple of parking tickets but no moving violations). Giving my license back to me, he said, "I'm gonna let you go with a warning this time. Just don't do it again." In that instance, I didn't get what I deserved: a ticket for making an illegal lane change. This exceptional police officer, whose name, if I could remember it, would be featured prominently here, decided to be kind to someone who had committed a traffic violation. He granted me mercy.

I'm sure you may have had a similar experience (or maybe you got that ticket I deserved; sorry). We've all, at one time or another, in one way or another, thrown ourselves on the mercy of the court. It may have been a traffic violation, forgetting a spouse's birthday, or something worse. We knew we deserved to be punished, but we hoped mercy would be extended.

Those who have problems with scripture or those who scoff at the idea of a God point to the Bible and continually talk about the fire and brimstone, about the anger and wrath of God. But there's a tremendous amount of mercy found in those pages, mercy that God extended to very undeserving individuals and nations. You just have to look.

In Genesis 6, we have the story of the flood, by which God destroyed humankind because of the sins of men and women. The mercy in that event is the time it took for Noah to build the ark, approximately one hundred years. While the Bible never explicitly tells us, we can assume Noah spent some of that time warning anyone who would listen that destruction was coming. Peter tells us in his second letter that Noah was "a preacher of righteousness." Surely, he spoke of God to others before the warning was issued and up until he and his family entered the ark. The mercy of God gave humankind time to repent. It was their choice.

The children of Israel were provided with God's mercy on many, many occasions. One such incident is found in Numbers 21. God had delivered the Canaanites to Israel in answer to a vow they had made to Him. Shortly after this, they were on a long journey and became so discouraged that they longed to be back in Egypt. At this point, God sent "fiery serpents" into the camp, and many of the people died. Their distress at this turn of events led them to plead with Moses to plead with God for them. So God told Moses to make an image of a fiery serpent and place it on a pole. Moses made the serpent. Anyone who was bitten need only look at the serpent to live. Those people who did look at the serpent lived. The crisis passed.

Now, some may say, "Aha, there's your wrath of God!" They would be correct. People died in the flood, but they were given the opportunity to escape. Israelites died because of the snakes, but when other Israelites repented and asked God for help, He gave it to them. God did not create the sin; the people engaged in the sin of their own free will. Genesis 6:5 tells us, "Every intent of the thoughts of [man's] heart was only evil continually" (NKJV). People were making up bad things to do, and their hearts were set on it—all the time. The children of Israel bellyached even after God had brought them out of Egypt and had given them a stunning victory.

But despite their sin and grumbling, God still loved them. He granted them mercy. It was up to them to take advantage of it. God was merciful to Rahab, but she was told to hang a red cord out of her window as a seal of her belief in that mercy. God was merciful to Naaman, but he had to dip seven times in the River Jordan to access that mercy. God was willing to be merciful to the people of Nineveh, but they had to admit their sin and turn from it to access that mercy.

In each of those cases and in all the others, that mercy was an extension of God's love. When Jesus says, "Be merciful as your Father in heaven is merciful," He means for us to follow these types of examples. God loves; God is merciful. That's what the *therefore* is there for—to put the two thoughts together.

If we're going to love our enemies (and friends), we must learn to demonstrate mercy to them, just as God shows His love and His mercy to us. We can't have one without the other. It's important. Do you want to know how important? Well, look at this statement from Paul in Romans 1:

> And even as they did not like to retain God in their knowledge, God gave them over to a debased mind, to do those things which are not fitting; being filled with all unrighteousness, sexual immorality, wickedness, covetousness, maliciousness; full of envy, murder, strife, deceit, evil-mindedness; they are whisperers, backbiters, haters of God, violent, proud, boasters, inventors of evil things, disobedient to parents, undiscerning, untrustworthy, unloving, unforgiving, unmerciful; who, knowing the righteous judgment of God, that those who practice such things are deserving of death, not only do the same but also approve of those who practice them. (Romans 1:28–32 NJKV)

The ones Paul is talking about in this passage are not filled with the immeasurable love and mercy of God; they're filled with all manner of evil, and one of the evils of these individuals is that they are unmerciful. Being unmerciful ranks right up there with some nasty sins, and the punishment is the same—the unmerciful are deserving of death. Mercy is important to God because it's part of who He is, and it must be part of who we are.

Some look at mercy as letting someone off the hook. Think of murderers sentenced to death who have had the sentence commuted to life in prison. Many who hear this news vehemently disagree with the commutation, saying, in essence, that the murderer got away with the crime and escaped punishment, as if spending the rest of your life behind bars is not that big a deal. A quick look in Genesis 4 dispels that myth. Cain murdered his brother Abel. When confronted with the deed, he, at first, tried to act as if he knew nothing (wouldn't you?), but eventually, God let him know that there was no escape from the truth. God—merciful God—did not strike Cain down at that moment, which, if you listen to some who think of God as cruel and heartless, would seem to be the way to handle the situation. Instead, He granted this murderer mercy; God commuted Cain's sentence to life—albeit a life as a fugitive and a vagabond. He would become someone who would no longer till the ground to raise his own crops but would depend on the kindness of others and his own resources to obtain what he needed.

Others look at mercy as allowing offenders or sinners to have their cake and eat it too, but this isn't true either. Okay, in some rare cases, it may be true. Some people have no conscience and feel no guilt at all, regardless of the situation. These people are known as sociopaths. Mercy has no effect on sociopaths' behavior; in fact, it will often embolden them to greater heights of offense. You can almost hear the person say, "Well, I got away with that one. What a pushover!" However, most people are not so vacant of feelings. In those quiet moments with their thoughts, the offense rises and jabs at the heart. In those moments, the memory of the hateful words or nasty deed nudges the conscience toward a feeling of guilt. Eventually, the guilt causes the person to act. Sometimes, the act is one of contrition. Sometimes, the person becomes more defensive and casts blame for the guilty feelings on the one who "caused" them—the person who was offended. In either case, it's mercy that can calm the heart of the guilty person and repair the rifts created by of the offense.

In Psalm 32, David writes a plaintive cry of repentance and thanksgiving to the Lord. His sin with Bathsheba and the murder of Uriah were fresh on his mind. At one point, he talks about how he felt when he stewed in the guilt of his sins; his bones felt old and worn out; he lashed out at others, and the guilt at what he had done rested heavily on his shoulders. But then, he acknowledged his sin, thanks in no small part to the prophet Nathan's urging, and God forgave him.

"Wait a minute," some might say, "David's son still died. That doesn't seem very merciful." Granted, on the surface, to you and me, it may not seem to be a nice thing to do. Certainly, many might think it very unmerciful to cause a child to suffer and die because of the sin of his mother and father. To that, I would have to ask this: "What would you have done?" Bear in mind that if you were making this decision, you would have been the one to say in Leviticus 10:20, "If a man commits adultery with another man's wife—with the wife of his neighbor—both the adulterer and the adulteress are to be put to death." Would you have left the child fatherless or motherless? Would you have executed David and Bathsheba before the child was born, killing an innocent child in the womb? Or would you have been the one to let them have their cake and eat it too?

It might do well to ask if God was actually being merciful to the child. Having died at only seven days old, the child was safe in the bosom of the Lord, in the presence of God, just as David intimated after the child's death. "Can I bring him back again? I shall go to him, but he shall not return to me," David said in 1 Samuel 12:23 (KJV). The child was spared decades of life on this earth, with all its intrigues and risks. Add to that the possible stigma attached to the circumstances and his birth, and you can see his life may not have been a bed of roses. True, he would have been the son of the king, but consider how things worked out years later with Absalom and David. This is all conjecture, of course, but we need to remember, as Paul points out in Romans 9, that God shows His mercy to whom He will in the manner and at the time He decides.

I'm not God; you're not God. But we can try to emulate His merciful nature as best we can. God wants us to be merciful and not just to those for whom we demonstrate that trait. Mercy isn't just intended for the recipient; it's intended for the giver.

Noted pastoral counselor Dr. Gregory Popcak said this: "Mercy is the virtue that allows us to address offenses in a manner that is mindful of the larger relationship and invites the offender into a deeper relationship with the offended. Obviously, that's going to require some work. The point is not that mercy lets people get away with an offense. It's that true mercy allows the addressing of the offense to be an opportunity for greater healing and unity by calling the person out in a way that makes both of you more whole."[2]

Salespeople and customer service representatives are trained to look for opportunities, even in a bad situation. Somewhere in the customer's comment is a little opening, just a word or a phrase, that gives the salesperson or customer service representative a chance to repair the damage and change a hostile call into a much better experience. When we're dealing with those who have wronged us or hurt us, we need to look for a way to turn the situation around. It may not be what we want to do, but showing God's mercy is a way to show God's love.

Now, sometimes it might actually mean we're letting the person get away with it, but in the long run, does it really matter that much? When you're talking about capital crimes, you might have a good argument. But let's be honest—most of the time, we're dealing with relationships with loved ones, friends, acquaintances, fellow employees, bank tellers, waiters, clerks at the department store, checkers at the grocery store, even brothers and sisters in Christ! In other words, we're dealing with those from whom we hope to get mercy when we do something wrong.

If we look at giving mercy to our enemies (you remember—the ones we're supposed to love) or to those who have offended us as an opportunity, instead of as giving others their just desserts, the result will be much better for all concerned. Believe it or not, giving mercy can make the person receiving that mercy feel loved. It can soften a heart, if only incrementally.

There's another side to mercy that we should mention at this point, one that God demonstrates just as much as the first side. A great example is found in Luke 7:

---

[2] Gregory Popcak, "What Does It Mean to 'Show Mercy'?," *Faith on the Couch* (blog), April 2, 2013.

Now it happened, the day after, that He went into a city called Nain; and many of His disciples went with Him, and a large crowd. And when He came near the gate of the city, behold, a dead man was being carried out, the only son of his mother; and she was a widow. And a large crowd from the city was with her. When the Lord saw her, He had compassion on her and said to her, "Do not weep." Then He came and touched the open coffin, and those who carried him stood still. And He said, "Young man, I say to you, arise." So he who was dead sat up and began to speak. And He presented him to his mother. (Luke 7:11–15 NKJV)

This story of raising the son of the widow of Nain from the dead is a perfect example of the merciful side of the Lord. That's because mercy isn't just *not* punishing us; it's also giving us blessings that we may not exactly deserve. In Psalm 23:6, David said, "Surely goodness and mercy shall follow me all the days of my life; and I will dwell in the house of the Lord forever" (NKJV). The Hebrew word for mercy is *checed*, and it's translated in many other passages as "kindness."

The same word was used when Abraham's servant was looking for a wife for Isaac. The servant prayed, "Show kindness to my master Abraham" (Genesis 24:12 NKJV).

The same word was used when Joseph pleaded with the butler to help him get out of prison. Joseph said, "But remember me when it is well with you, and please show kindness to me; make mention of me to Pharaoh, and get me out of this house" (Genesis 40:14 NKJV).

It was used when Ruth showed kindness and mercy to her future husband, Boaz, and when David showed kindness to Mephibosheth, Jonathan's son.

In those cases and in many others, mercy was a gift of kindness, which is another type of mercy we are commanded to demonstrate. Think of it as a preemptive attack against Satan; it's a way of reaching out to someone to bless him or her by sharing the blessing of mercy God has given us.

Jesus saw the widow of Nain slowly marching in the funeral procession. He saw the pain on her face and understood the ache in her soul, and He decided, for whatever reason, to give her a miraculous gift—the renewed life of her son. Why did Jesus choose to help this poor woman? Maybe it was to show His power and authority, or maybe it was to show the empathy that God has for those who suffer. A couple of years later, when they heard about Jesus rising from the dead, how do you think they felt?

Yes, some may say we're showing weakness or being pushovers when we give mercy. Has someone to whom you've been merciful ever taken advantage of you? Has giving mercy cost you time, money, or embarrassment? We've all experienced it once or twice, but in the end, does it really matter if people think we're pushovers or if someone does take advantage of us? We know we're not pushovers; we know why we're doing it. What do we get? We get the satisfaction of knowing God knows, and in the end, He's the only one who matters. Can we give mercy? Yes! We can give mercy if we'll allow God to control the giving, allow Him to guide our words, allow Him to soften our hearts, and allow mercy to surround others as it surrounds us.

Just as love should be unconditional, mercy should have no strings attached. The command from Jesus is to "be merciful *as* your Father in heaven is merciful." I think this may be why Jesus made His next comment: "Judge not, and you shall not be judged. Condemn not, and you shall not be condemned."

Wow, where do we go with this? It is the one verse that even atheists will pull out of scripture to bolster any position. Most often, people will dip back into Matthew 7:1 and use the statement Jesus made during the Sermon on the Mount: "Judge not, that you be not judged" (NKJV). But they'll also allude to this verse, where Jesus tacks on the "condemn not." Back in Matthew, Jesus also told us to consider the plank in our own eyes before we consider the speck in someone else's eye. "Look," the reasoning goes, "even Jesus said not to judge me because you've got so much sin in your own life. Who are you to tell me I can't _____?" The implication is that no one—absolutely no one (especially Christians)—should judge anyone else.

Let's parse this a little because it's evident that the world is not getting the real message here. This thought has been used to mask and excuse all manner of evil and sin at least since the days of Moses. You remember the incident: Moses saw an Egyptian beating an Israelite. He waited until no one could see, killed the Egyptian, and hid the body in the sand. The next day, he saw two Israelites fighting and demanded to know of the one who was in the wrong, "Why are you striking your companion?" The answer from one of the Israelites was, "Who made you a prince and a judge?" Never mind that the Israelite was in the wrong; he was upset because someone pointed it out, and he tried to excuse it by calling attention to the sin that Moses had committed.

What was that first equation our parents tried to teach us? I think it was, "Two wrongs don't make a right." The Israelite was still guilty, and it may well have been his guilt over the incident that caused him to lash out at Moses. Interestingly, many of the people who use the "two wrongs" phrase will use this same justification when someone talks to them about a wrong. "Judge not," they'll say. "Look at the plank in your own eye!" Well, you have me there. I may not have murdered an Egyptian, but I have, in the past, had planks in my eye. However, as happens most times, those who quote this scripture tend to leave out the last part. After addressing the plank in your own eye, you will then, as Jesus plainly states, "see clearly to remove the speck from your brother's eye." The speck, the sin, is still there in my brother's eye. If I take care of the sin in my own life, I am better prepared to help you take care of the sin in yours. It's called *experience*.

Once I experience the mercy of God and His forgiveness, which we'll talk about shortly, I can use my experience with sin to assist you in extricating it from your life. It happens all the time in the secular world, and no one gets upset about it. What do you think goes on in Alcoholics Anonymous, Al-Anon, Nar-Anon, and similar organizations? There's a tremendous amount of judging that goes on within the members of those groups. Those who've been entrapped by alcohol or drugs or sex can spot someone who's just mouthing the words a mile away, and they will basically say something along the lines of, "Come back when you're serious."

Now, all that being said, Jesus does say that we should not judge, and we should not condemn. But what is it we shouldn't judge or condemn? I believe that here in Luke and in the companion passages, Jesus is telling us not to judge the attitude, not to judge the heart of the person. He's telling us not to condemn based solely on the actions. He's really telling us not to condemn at all because that's not our job. If you see Miss Scarlet murder Mr. Boddy in the hall with the lead pipe, and you're called as a witness, the moment you point to the lady in red and say, "She did it," you are judging her actions; you are saying she is a murderer, which she is! But if you judge her heart and condemn her soul based only on this one act, you've gone against the word of Jesus. Of course, this doesn't mean you have to set her free to go after Colonel Mustard with the wrench; she still must pay for her crime. Depending on the circumstances, Miss Scarlet may spend a considerable amount of time in jail or even have to pay with her own life. Who knows, though, if God may have placed you in the situation to help Miss Scarlet come to know the Lord?

That, I believe, is why Jesus placed this statement where He did. If we're going to be merciful, we have to learn how to be graceful. I can certainly judge if an action is wrong, based on a standard; that's what we sometimes call "righteous judgment." I can condemn the act as a sin or evil. But I cannot, according to Jesus, judge the person or the intent of his or her heart, nor can I condemn the person. If I do that, I'm moving into dangerous territory. As a matter of fact, in the Matthew 7 passage, Jesus also adds this warning: "For with what judgment you judge, you will be judged; and with the measure you use, it will be measured back to you."

Let's be clear, though; the caution Jesus commanded against judging does not mean that I overlook the sin, nor does it mean I tolerate or excuse the sin. What it means is, I look at the sinner (here, I say, as Paul said, "of whom I am the worst") through God's eyes, through a prism of mercy and grace. I hope the sinner looks at me through those same eyes.

The second attribute of God that Jesus tells us is essential is forgiveness. "Forgive, and you will be forgiven."

There's a progression in the commands Jesus made in Luke 6. It began with love your enemies; allow the immeasurable love of God to cascade over the lives of others by loving them with His love. If we're loving them with His love, we'll show mercy; we'll learn to be graceful, and, if all goes well, we'll learn to forgive.

This may well be the toughest part of His statements in Luke 6, the most difficult to hear and the one even more difficult to perform. We can learn to love people, even those we once considered unlovable. We can learn to get beyond wrongs from the past, to put them on the back burner in the spirit of comradeship. But forgiveness is something entirely different. Forgiveness is something we're very stingy with, or maybe we're just more selective—or maybe it's a little of both. Forgiveness is something we parcel out following very strict guidelines. The problem is, they're our guidelines, not the Lord's.

We're all a little like Peter. "How often should I forgive someone who sins against me?" Peter asks in Matthew 18. "Up to seven times?" Now, that seems a fairly reasonable number. If someone steals from me, then repents, and I forgive him, I've done well. If the same person does it five more times, and I forgive, that's good too. But if he does it again—well, at some point there has to be a last straw, and seven times should be the point at which I will say, "No, I can't forgive you!"

But Jesus has an answer that neither Peter nor we are expecting. "I do not say to you, up to seven times, but up to seventy times seven." I like to think at that point Peter blinked a couple of times and let out a long, low whistle. "That's a lot of forgiveness. I thought I was being pretty generous with seven times. Now you're telling me 490? Wow!"

It's at this point, Jesus tells the fairly transparent parable of the servant who owed ten thousand talents to a king. Modern scholars tell us ten thousand talents is equal to several million dollars in today's money. No wonder the servant begged for patience when called to account! The king, in a moment of compassion, went beyond simply having patience by forgiving the entire debt. Interestingly, Jesus doesn't say anything about the man thanking the king, but shortly thereafter, the servant finds a man who owes him one hundred denarii (about $160). He grabs the man by the throat and demands payment. The man falls before the servant and begs for patience, but the servant has the man cast into debtor's prison "till he should pay the debt." Upon hearing of this turn of events, the king calls the servant before him. He is not happy. "You wicked servant," the king says, "I forgave you all that debt because you begged me. Should you not also have had compassion on your fellow servant, just as I had pity on you?" The king then has the servant taken to the torturers, not just debtor's prison, until the servant pays everything due to the king.

Jesus closes the parable with these words: "So My heavenly Father also will do to you if each of you, from his heart, does not forgive his brother his trespasses." The implication here is that we must forgive, we must forgive whenever we're asked, and we must put no limit on the number of times that someone can ask our forgiveness and have it granted. In addition, the forgiveness can't be just words; emotions must be involved as well. We must really mean it.

When I reread the previous paragraph, I had to let out a long, low whistle myself. That's quite a challenge. Now, you would think giving forgiveness would be something we'd all want to do, considering we've been forgiven by God for all we've done, but you would be wrong. Oh, we can say, "I forgive you," all day long, but meaning it, saying it from the heart, is quite another matter.

The Greek word Jesus uses for heart in the Matthew 18:35 passage is *kardia*. It does refer to that life-giving organ beating in our chests, but *Strong's Concordance* also gives other definitions: "the center and seat of spiritual life—the soul or mind, as it is the fountain and seat of the thoughts, passions, desires, appetites, affections, purposes, endeavors; of the understanding, the faculty and seat of the intelligence; of the will and character; of the soul so far as it is affected and stirred in a bad way or good, or of the soul as the seat of the sensibilities, affections, emotions, desires, appetites, passions."

This is the same word Jesus used when He told the scribe to "love the Lord with all your heart, with all your soul, with all your mind, and with all your strength." Forgiveness requires that much passion; it requires that much emotion. There is little doubt Jesus wants us to forgive from the very core of our beings as often as someone asks for that forgiveness.

Webster's Dictionary defines *forgive* as, "to cease to feel resentment against an offender." Forgiveness is the act of forgiving. If only it were that simple. The Greek word used by Jesus in these two instances and the one used most often in the New Testament is *apolyō*. This word goes much deeper than just ceasing to have resentment against someone who has wronged us. According to *Strong's Concordance*, *apolyō* means, "To set free; to let go, dismiss, to bid depart, send away; to let go free, release, said of a captive to release his bonds, give liberty; to acquit one accused of a crime; indulgently, to grant a prisoner leave to depart; to release a debtor."

Now, what's the sense you get from the word *forgiveness*? Would you agree that it has to do with setting people free, releasing them from their bondage? But what is that bondage?

This is the way it usually happens: My coworker wrongs me, and I take offense; I'm filled with indignation. He later realizes the wrong and apologizes. "No problem," I answer. There's an awkward silence before he half smiles, then walks away, wondering if all really is well. I watch, knowing I've taken the high road and knowing I've been magnanimous in casting my forgiveness out there for him and everyone else to see. Meanwhile, I continue to wallow in my anger and to cling to the grudge that I've gathered in my arms. If I'm lucky, I can carry it for a long time. Even though it gets heavier and heavier, I just won't give it up. Sometimes, it seems as if I enjoy being slighted and revel in allowing him to carry a little extra guilt around in his life, while at the same time, I struggle to carry my burden. But it just feels so good to hurt so bad, to have someone else share my hurt, especially since he was the one who caused it in the first place!

As a very good friend of mine said, "It's as if we're saying, 'How dare you not feel heartbroken for hurting me!'" We think we can't let it go, when the truth is, we don't want the other person to let it go. How sad that I can't set my heart free from the bondage of its hurt and can't release my coworker from the bondage of guilt he feels for what's been done. How sad that both of us are imprisoned by my selfishness. Make no mistake about it: not forgiving is a sign of selfishness. It's all about me; it's all about how my feelings have been hurt and all about how I feel. Forgiving from the heart means I have to put all that aside and stop being selfish. Forgiving means I have to swallow my pride and put my trust in the Lord and in the person who slighted me.

Here's an amazing thing: When something bad happens to your average Christian, he or she will say, "I'm going to put my trust in the Lord to get me through this. I know there's a purpose to it all." Yet when your average Christian is offended, he or she has a tough time saying the same thing. They'll say, "But just listen to what they did or said!" But Jesus says, "It doesn't matter; forgive—as I forgave." Not to be flip, but do you really think as Jesus was hanging on the cross and said, "Father, forgive them," He really meant, "Hey, no problem guys"? Do you honestly believe any offense you've taken or hurt you've experienced at the hand of another compares to being executed in a cruel, inhumane, and unjust way by people who hated you because you taught them the truth?

In Luke 7:36 and following, we find a wonderful forgiveness story. Jesus is having dinner with a Pharisee named Simon when a woman—a "sinner," the scripture tells us—comes into the house and approaches Him. She's weeping, obviously overcome by her sinful life, and the tears come so fast and heavy that she is able to wash the feet of Jesus with them. Then, she wipes the feet with her hair and kisses them. After this, she pours an alabaster flask of oil on His feet.

The Pharisee looks askance at the scene but says nothing out loud. In his thoughts, he wonders, *If this man really is a prophet, He would know what kind of woman this is … a sinner!*

At this point, Jesus asks the Pharisee for his opinion about a subject. A creditor has two debtors: one owes him five hundred denarii; the other owes fifty. Neither can pay, so the creditor forgives both of them their debts. "Which of them will love him more?" Jesus asks. The answer is fairly simple.

"I suppose the one whom he forgave more," the Pharisee answers.

"You have rightly judged," Jesus says. You can almost see a faint smile come to His face as He continues the lesson.

Turning to look at the woman, Jesus explains to Simon that the woman washed His feet, kissed them, and anointed them with oil while he, Simon, had not given Jesus water, kissed Him in greeting, or anointed Him with soothing oil. Then He says, "Therefore ... her sins, which are many, are forgiven, for she loved much. But to whom little is forgiven, the same loves little."

Apparently, the woman had heard Jesus speaking or had heard about Him. She was moved to seek Him out and to offer Him honor and respect. The scripture doesn't say that she wanted anything from Jesus, only that she was overcome with emotion, which came out as tears to wash His feet, hair to dry them, and a fragrant oil to anoint them. In Luke's account, we don't know the woman's name; we don't know why she was considered such a sinner, and maybe that's the whole point. She could be me; she could be you. She came to Jesus with a broken heart. She came with a changed heart.

Jesus, whose heart is always open to the sinner who humbly approaches Him, forgave her with no questions asked and no strings attached. It must have been difficult for her to believe because He ended up having to tell her three times!

But what of Simon? Well, Simon had some work to do; his reaction was like ours is sometimes: "This woman has a lot of baggage. Who does she think she is, coming before Jesus, and who does He think He is, letting her touch Him?" This woman, as far as we know, had done nothing to hurt or slight Simon, other than to appear at his house, uninvited, and interrupt his time with Jesus. When you boil it down to its essence, the only thing this woman did to Simon was offend his sensibilities. How sad that Simon couldn't even have compassion for a weeping woman who was obviously overcome by her emotions. Instead, he only thought of himself.

I do think it's a bit ironic that when Simon answers Jesus about which debtor would love the creditor more, Jesus answers, "You have rightly judged." It's the same word He used in Luke 6 when talking about forgiveness: "Judge not, and you will not be judged." To further add to the irony in the situation, Jesus point-blank judges Simon. Look closely at what He says:

"Do you see this woman? I entered your house; you gave Me no water for My feet, but she has washed My feet with her tears and wiped them with the hair of her head. You gave Me no kiss, but this woman has not ceased to kiss My feet since the time I came in. You did not anoint My head with oil, but this woman has anointed My feet with fragrant oil. Therefore I say to you, her sins, which are many, are forgiven, for she loved much. But to whom little is forgiven, the same loves little." (Luke 7:44–47 NKJV)

Jesus intimates that Simon has not learned to forgive, nor has he learned to love. Simon's heart was not changed, so he could not learn to love as God or to forgive as God. Yes, Simon had a lot of work to do but no more than we all have to do.

Forgiveness takes a change of heart. Surprisingly, though, the change of heart isn't just on the offender; it's on the offended as well. It's through the change of heart that the offender may come to learn how to change his or her heart.

Learning to forgive is a difficult task. It's something we all struggle with. It's something we try to skirt sometimes because of its difficulty. But it's an action we must learn and a trait we must cultivate. If we're to be filled with God's immeasurable love, it's going to also take the form of His immeasurable mercy and forgiveness.

"I can do all things through Christ who strengthens me," Paul tells us. You can give forgiveness. You can give mercy. You can give love. Yes, you can do it all because it is Christ who gives you the strength to say, "I love you no matter what you did. I won't try to get back at you, regardless of what you did. I will forgive you, no matter how much you hurt me."

When typewriters first came to general use, mistakes were corrected using the good old eraser. That instrument left a lot of smudges, never really completely got rid of the mistake, and sometimes destroyed the paper. Liquid Paper was invented back in the late '50s by a secretary named Betty Nesmith. She developed it in her kitchen because she was tired of erasing her mistakes. Liquid Paper would cover it completely! But there was still that blob of white showing on the paper to let everyone know that an error had been made. In the '60s, erase ribbons came along. They got rid of the errors more effectively, but there were still the impressions of the original imprint if you looked close enough. Now, we have the delete key! Don't like what you wrote? Delete, delete, delete, delete—it's gone!

When it comes to forgiveness, we often use the first method—we forgive, but the memory is still there. God uses the delete key when He forgives. When it comes to forgiveness, forget the Liquid Paper or erase ribbons. Instead, move into the computer age and use that delete key so that where the error was will now be a blank space, ready to have something new and better added to the story.

If we can learn to do this, this is the promise Jesus makes: "Give, and it will be given to you: a good measure, pressed down, shaken together, and running over will be put into your bosom." The more forgiveness I give, the more I'll get. The more mercy I give, the more I'll get. The more love I give, the more I'll get—the more hope I will have.

PART 3

Fill Your Heart with Hope

9

The Journal

Then the Lord saw that the wickedness of man was great in the earth.

—Genesis 6:5 (NKJV)

When you're at the end of your rope, tie a knot and hold on.

—Theodore Roosevelt

These are the last words that I shall ever write.

They are written with an overpowering fear of what lies ahead. These are feelings I've never before experienced. But in the last month, they have become my constant companions, leaning over my shoulder every waking hour. And there are oh so many of those.

Once I was the master of a village. When there was a decision to be made, the people came to me, for I was the wisest man they knew. I conducted the marriage ceremonies, led the funerals, and blessed new babies. The villagers looked up to me and respected me; they even feared me. My family and I had the greatest house, the best clothing, the finest food. Now, we wear only what we have on our backs. We eat what little we can find along the ground.

What of our great house? It is gone. So is the village. Yes, every stone of every house, every barn, every fence, every field, all our livestock, food, clothing—all those possessions we in the village have spent a lifetime gathering. Everything is gone. Everything lies at the bottom of an ever-increasing sea. It is ever increasing because this thing he called "rain" just will not stop.

Now, I must tell this story before it is too late.

There was a man named Noah who lived near our village. He was a good man and a hard worker. We wanted him and his family involved with our community. Time and again, they were invited to harvest feasts, new moon feasts, and all our parties and reveling, but Noah always refused. He told us he could not worship our gods. Because of this, some of the more vocal villagers found it necessary to hurl insults Noah's way whenever he came around; others, I believe, may have hurled more than that. But the majority of us eventually just ignored him.

Our village continued its feasts, festivals, and orgies. Noah and his family continued their quiet, dull, and sleepy existence.

Then one day, many years ago, unusual activities began around Noah's farm. He and his sons made journey after journey to a nearby forest, coming back each time with immense loads of freshly hewn gopher wood. Ordinarily, we would have continued to ignore them, but the sheer number of trips and the size of the return loads lent an air of mystery to their project. As the first outline of the structure was laid, the mystery deepened.

Several times each month, we took turns traveling to the hill overlooking Noah's farm to watch the progress. First, a lattice-work frame was constructed in an immense open area near the family house. We could not believe the size of the frame—over four hundred feet long, seventy-five or eighty feet wide. When this frame was finished, they began the next phase. A smaller section was built, and they joined boards together as a wall. The section was stood on its end, and pitch was applied to both sides. They were certainly making the walls strong, we thought. But after several of the sides had dried, they laid them out on top of the frame. They were making a floor! It was truly unusual to waste wood on a floor. Rumors flew.

"It is a barn for his crops," someone said at our next village meeting.

"Maybe it is a new house for his family," yet another suggested.

"For eight people?" was the question.

"It must be a temple," stated one of our elders, "a temple for that God he worships. Perhaps he makes it so big because he thinks he can convince us to join him!"

That brought a fresh round of derisive laughter. But Noah was not there to hear it; he and his sons were beginning the walls of the building.

Year by year, they made slow, steady progress. When they reached around ten feet in height, they set columns on the floor; then they built another floor section. This continued until three separate floors were finished. Finally, they began what appeared to be the roof. It was then that my curiosity overcame my dislike of Noah, and I went to find out just what was being built.

I slowly made my way up the now well-worn pathway to the building site. The midday sun was beating mercilessly down; heat rose rapidly, inviting a soothing period of sleep. But Noah and his family showed no signs of taking a rest. They worked as only those with a true purpose can work.

His wife and daughters-in-law were busy over two separate fires. Two of the women were working with a boiling cauldron full of pitching material; the other two were preparing what looked to be a meager midday meal. The men were working on the structure itself. Noah, Ham, and Shem were straining on a rope, lifting yet another floor section toward the fourth level. Japheth stood on the framework, ready to receive the cargo. As the heavy flooring was finally lifted to his level, he caught a glimpse of me approaching. His task was momentarily forgotten as he stared at me, a mixture of disbelief and disdain on his face.

"Japheth," Noah called, "we cannot hold this much longer. Get your mind out of the sky and back to your duties."

Silently, Japheth raised a hand and pointed my way. The women stopped their work and looked; Noah and his two other sons stole quick glances over their shoulders. All was quiet now, save for the boiling pots, as eight pairs of eyes studied my slow, deliberate steps.

At last, Noah turned back to the rope. "Japheth," he called again.

All three sons turned their attention to their father. "Secure the flooring before this rope or our muscles give way."

Japheth obediently swung the flooring into place, loosening the harness that had been used to raise it. He let that piece fall and busied himself installing the flooring.

Noah let go of the rope and, wiping his hands on his robe, turned toward me. By then, I was standing beside him.

"Greetings, Noah," I said.

"And greetings to you," he answered.

I was staring at the structure. From the hilltop it had looked immense. Standing so close made it seem overpowering. Never had I seen a man-made object so large.

"Impressive, Noah," I finally managed to whisper, "very impressive. But—"

He read my thoughts, of course. "But what is it?" he finished for me.

Slowly turning to face him, I could only smile.

"We have seen all of you watching us for some time," he said. "We knew someone would eventually feel compelled to come and find out what this is. But—"

"But"—it was my turn to interrupt—"you never expected me." He nodded. I returned my attention to the structure. Slowly I followed its frame from one end to the other, from top to bottom. Then I looked at Noah again. "What is it?" I asked.

"It is an ark," he said quietly.

I raised my eyebrows in astonishment. "An ark?" I replied. Again, he nodded. "Noah, you realize you are quite a distant journey from the nearest water. Perhaps you should have—"

He held up his hand. "We do not intend to take this to the river, nor is it intended for a pleasure journey," he announced.

"What then?" I asked

"It is for the destruction to come."

"The destruction to come?" I asked. I could not understand what that statement meant. It made no sense. "What do you mean by that?"

Noah looked at me, eyes aglow; then he told me the most amazing story I have ever heard.

"One day, many years past, I was in my fields, tilling. Suddenly, I heard my name called. I looked around, but I could see no one. And then the voice came again. 'Noah,' it said, 'you have found grace in my eyes.'

"'Who are you?' I asked.

"And the voice answered simply, 'I am the Lord your God.'

"Immediately, I fell to my knees. 'My Lord, I am your humble servant. What would you have me to do?'

"His voice was quiet, calm in its tone. Yet I could feel the resolve behind it. 'Noah, I am sorry that I ever made mankind. They have turned their faces away from me; they have begun to take part in every manner of evil, and I know they will never return to me. Therefore, I shall bring a great flood upon all the earth and wash it clean. But you and your family alone, I shall save. Because you have found grace in my eyes.'

"I was dumbstruck, I could only listen as He instructed me on what to do. He told me to build this ark. He gave me the exact size to make it and told me what materials to use. When we are done with this, we shall place males and females of all the animals on board. Then I, my wife, my sons, and their wives will board."

Noah's voice trailed off as he finished the story. He turned back to watch the work his sons were doing on the ark.

"And then?" I asked.

"And then God will flood this earth and destroy it—all that is in it; all that is on it," he replied quietly.

I began to laugh. Uncontrollably. "Flood the earth?" I said, after I had calmed down some. "A good tale, Noah. Perhaps you could come tell it around the fire some night."

Noah frowned. "I will come talk around the fire," he said, "but this is no tale, my friend. God will destroy this earth. He is tired of the orgies, the murders, the disrespect—the disbelief."

"All our 'evils,'" I sneered.

"Yes."

"And you will be saved in this ark?"

"Yes, I, my family"—here, he paused, then spread his hands out to continue—"and anyone else who will turn from the world back to God."

There was a long silence after that, one in which I contemplated all that Noah had said. It was an amazing story but a preposterous one. Still, there was something about the way he told it. He was convincing.

"And how did you say God will destroy the earth?" I asked.

"He will open the fountains of the earth. And he will cause it to rain."

There was a word I had never heard before: *rain*. I asked what that was. He did not know.

"I do not question the words of God," he said. "I do not understand everything He tells me, nor do I know why He tells me the things He does. I only know there is but one course to follow: obedience."

I laughed again. "Blind faith! Blind trust! Blind obedience! You do not understand things He says. You do not know why you obey, but you just do. Why, Father Noah"—I looked at him with a smile of triumph—"you are no more than a dog. 'Fetch,' God says. 'Heel,' He commands, and you wag your tail and obey."

"An interesting comparison," Noah answered. His face did not change expression as he continued. "But tell me, Elder, when you command your child to fetch firewood, does he question you?"

"Not if he wishes to continue standing," I declared.

"Ah, yes. Your wife, of course, understands you wish dinner at a certain point in the evening." I nodded; he continued. "I'm sure those who live in your village know that your orders are the orders that must be followed, no matter what."

Again, I nodded. "But Noah, I am the village elder, the father of the child, and the head of the house. I must be obeyed!"

A smile came across Noah's face for the first time since I had arrived. "And so is the Lord. He too must be obeyed," he whispered.

I could only shake my head in wonder. "If my child fails to obey me, he feels my wrath. He knows I am there watching him. He can see me, touch me, and know me." I paused and once again looked Noah in the eyes. "Show me God," I said.

Noah lifted his hand and pointed to the mountains in the distance.

"He is there," he said. Then, he looked to the sky. "And there." He stooped to pick a wildflower. "And He is here. The Lord is in all and through all. He makes the sun to shine and the moon to rise. The wind is His breath; the birds are His song. You can see God in the beauty of a sunset; you touch Him in the warmth of a child's hand. You can know the Lord in the joy of doing His will. God made this world from nothing." He paused and pointed to his chest. "But most of all, God is here, in the heart. His love and grace lives in the heart that follows Him, that longs to do the will of God and keep himself free from sin and evil. But now the evils of mankind have made of this world nothing. So He has decided to cleanse it. And He will."

I could only stare at him in stunned silence. Then, I finally sighed heavily. "You speak of beauty and joy, of love and grace, and then you tell me that your God is going to kill us all."

"No," he answered. "He has told me that He is tired of the evil and sin. He has told me that He is going to destroy this world, but He has also told me that He cares." Noah looked into my eyes with a piercing gaze now. "He has offered a way to escape the destruction. For my family and me—and for anyone who will turn back to Him."

I returned his gaze, and we stood that way for several moments. Finally, I turned to look at the ark. Noah's sons were lifting more flooring and putting it in place. I then watched the four women as they busied themselves, finishing the noon meal and tending to the boiling pitch. Finally, my eyes returned to Noah. I expected to see a cold, angry expression. Instead, I saw only compassion, concern, and caring.

"Noah, I believe you are a madman," was all I could think to say.

His response was short. "I believe I am a saved man."

I turned to leave without comment. How could I further reason with a man who had lost his senses? As I walked back down the pathway, he called after me.

"I shall come to your village and preach my message to the people."

I made no response; I only walked away. That evening, during our village meeting, I told everyone what Noah had told me. Such laughter had never been heard before, nor will it ever be heard again.

Several days later, Noah himself appeared and tried to speak.

Villagers drifted in and out of the meeting circle, shaking their heads, laughing, and casting insults at him.

The only ones who really listened were the children. Ah, the children—innocent, open, and ultimately terrified by his tale of destruction. That was enough for us. He was banned from the village from that time on. So he and his family finished the ark. Many times, he would again try to warn fellow villagers individually, but no one listened.

And then one day, the most amazing event of all occurred. Animals of every kind began roaming onto Noah's land, animals none of us had ever seen before. They came slowly, almost casually. Hooves clopped through the dust; all manner of animal calls mixed in a fantastic chorus of sounds! They did not stop till they reached the ark. There, they stood, almost patiently, as Noah and the others led them, two by two, up the ramp and into the dark recesses of the vessel.

We villagers—I include myself among them—ran to the hill overlooking the valley and watched it all with puzzled expressions. None of us could offer an explanation for this event. We stood watching for a long time; then, many of the others turned and went back to the village, leaving behind the strange sight.

However, I stayed and watched Noah and his family load the ark.

Dealing with the wild array of animals took the rest to the day and two more. They toiled in the blistering sun; they worked through the nights. Finally, only beasts of burden were left. They used those animals to load provisions. Barrel after barrel and bag after bag were slowly taken onto the ark. It was obvious that they had been holding back these necessities for some time, and it was obvious from the column of supplies that they expected to be in the ark for a long, long time.

By the fifth day, it appeared that all was ready. Ham, Shem, and Japheth conducted a last search of the house and work areas, collecting things that had been left behind. Then, they and their wives made their way up the ramp and disappeared into the darkness. Noah came to the doorway from inside.

A beautiful sun shone in a deep-blue sky. The only sounds that could be heard were the far-off songs of birds, one of those things Noah had used as evidence of his God on that long-ago day. Now, he stood at the doorway of the ark and looked at me once again. Yes, there were many of us standing on that hill, watching, but I am certain he meant his next gesture for me. It was an open hand. It was outstretched and motioning to come to the ark.

For a moment, my mind raced through the possibilities. What if he was right? What if there was a God, and what if He truly was going to destroy the world? Here, I stood on a hill; down in the valley was safety. I could feel my heart beating wildly in my chest. My hands were wet with perspiration. My mind willed my legs to move toward the ark, toward safety.

But then someone began to laugh. Then someone else joined in. More and more began to laugh loudly. Then the insults and taunts began.

My resolve went away. What had I been thinking? Had I gone into the ark, I was certain I would have come out in a few days, and I would have become the target of the laughter and insults. I would have lost the respect of my village and my position. In anger and frustration, I reached down for a stone. With all my strength, I threw it toward Noah. It fell far short of its mark. Others followed my example, though, heaving stones, sticks, and pebbles. Some moved farther down the hill to gain accuracy. Soon, some stones began hitting the side of the ark. The group was quickly becoming an angry mob, threatening any moment to rush down into the valley and physically take Noah. Calmer now, I called a halt to the scene. I had no desire to harm the man. Little did I know there was no way anything that I could do would harm Noah, his family, or his mission.

Through all this, Noah had continued to stand in the doorway and motion. He did not seem to mind that he might be struck by a stone at any moment. I remember thinking at the time that he was, in some way, taunting us. Now I know different. Despite all we had said and done to him, he still wanted us to join him and be saved.

By this time, Noah's entire family, curious about the uproar, had joined him at the doorway. They silently looked at us; we silently looked back. As we stared solemnly at each other, something very strange happened.

The door closed—by itself!

The discussion began there and continued that night around the fire. "Magic," one said. "Someone else in the ark," said another. Many different explanations were offered, but I am not sure any were believed. A strange sense of unease settled over the whole village. Mothers hugged their children closer. Fathers, who usually cajoled around the fire till late, went to their dwellings early. The village, usually vibrant and alive at all hours, was quiet through that first of many long nights. I retired early, and after many hours of restlessness, I finally drifted off to sleep.

My youngest son's small hand tapped lightly on my shoulder. I slowly emerged from the haze of slumber to the sound of his voice. "Father," he whispered. "Father."

Shaking off the last vestiges of sleep, I turned toward him. He pulled his hand back and looked at me with fearful eyes. But I could tell the fear was not of waking me.

"What is it, son?"

He pointed to the door. "Come and see, Father."

I slowly followed him to the door and looked out. When I saw the sky, I understood my son's fear; the sun was not there. Instead, the entire sky was gray. As we stood and watched, a bright flash of light traced a path from the clouds to the top of a hill not far from our village. This was followed by a low rumble that made pottery shake on the shelves in our house.

"That's what happened before," said my son. "What is it? Where is the sun?"

I turned to look at him. His lips trembled; tears welled in his eyes. I wanted to answer him, to reassure him that all was well. But there was no one to answer my questions, to reassure me.

And then water began to fall from the sky! It fell slowly at first, then it came down with an ever-quickening pace. The sound of the drops striking the ground, trees, and roofs grew louder and louder.

By now, my wife and other children were standing with us at the doorway. It was obvious that they too were frightened. With each flash of light and loud rumble, I could almost feel them trembling. I looked at each member of my family, smiling as best I could. They only stared back with fear-filled, questioning eyes.

Turning my attention to the rest of the village, I could see others also standing in the doorways. All were afraid to venture out, and all were looking in my direction. The tension grew, and the fear threatened to strangle us all. Everyone looked to me for an explanation. There was only one thing to do.

I took a step outside.

The water was cold, and the wind blowing across my quickly soaked skin made me even colder. I turned my face toward the sky and opened my mouth. The water tasted wonderful, fresh, and cool.

"It is a new gift from the gods," I announced to the village. "Come and enjoy it."

Villagers looked one to another, unsure of what to do at first. Then, my son came out. He followed my path and copied my movements, even tasting the water. Others emerged from their homes and joined us. Soon, the entire village was enjoying the new gift. For the next few days, we all played in it and used it as a new source of drinking water. But our joy soon waned, and our fear returned.

The water fell day and night, relentless in its pace. Streams began to overflow their banks; fields flooded, washing crops away. Our village, which sat on a small rise, was quickly coming into peril.

A council session was held. We decided to sacrifice to the gods. As village chief, I offered my oldest daughter. It was to no avail; the water would not stop.

Two days later, my wife came to me with tear-filled eyes. "We have given our daughter in vain," she said quietly.

"It appears so," I answered, staring out the doorway.

There was a long pause. When I finally turned to look at her, there was nothing but hatred in her eyes. "You are a fool," she spat at me. I raised my hand to pay her for her insult, but she did not move. "Go on; strike me down," she said. "I do not care. I do not fear you any longer. We are all doomed. You could have saved us all."

"How could I have saved us from this?" I asked, pointing outside.

"By listening to Noah," she answered through clenched teeth. "He and his family sit safe in their ark while all of us sit and await destruction."

I shook my head in disbelief. "Woman, you are the fool," I said.

"You did not seem to think so that day Noah entered the ark," she sneered. I began to protest, but she would not let me. "I have lived with you long enough to know your fears and to almost read your thoughts. You wanted to believe what Noah had said; there was doubt in your eyes. You even took a step. If you had gone to Noah, we would all be safe and dry."

"Had I done that, we would have been laughed at by everyone. We would have been cast out of the village."

She shook her head and sighed deeply. "The sky water falls day and night. The river has flooded our fields. Our daughter is dead, and still, you are filled with pride; still, you will not admit your failings. Had you gone to Noah and promised this God that we would turn from our evils, most would have followed you. Only a few would have laughed. But they would be here, while we would be safe in the ark."

"This falling water cannot last. We are not doomed, woman."

"Your words are full of courage. But your expressions betray you."

She was right, of course. Worry was etched deeply in my face, as it was in hers. "I had hoped to appease the gods with the sacrifice of our daughter," I finally said with a heavy sigh.

My wife laughed. "Gods? Gods? There are no 'gods'! There is only one God—Noah's God!"

I turned to stare out the door again. The water seemed to fall faster and faster, adding more to the puddles, which were quickly becoming ponds. My wife and I stood for a long while, watching friends and neighbors scurry from house to house. We saw some of them look up to the sky and curse. We saw the horror in their eyes.

At last, I turned back to her. "My wife, I believe it is time we finally admit one fact." She looked at me, the hatred now gone. "He is not just Noah's God," I said. "He is also our God."

That night, we held a council session and decided to flee the village for the mountain, that distant mountain Noah had pointed to not so long ago. The next morning, our journey began.

Our path took us past the site of Noah's ark. There, several villagers decided to plead with Noah to let us aboard. They waded to the ark and beat on the side, calling Noah's name. Despite hours of pleading, the door never opened. Finally, the group came back. Some cursed Noah; others cursed God. Some cursed both, calling them cruel and heartless. They asked what sort of God would care so little for His people to destroy them without a thought.

Ah, but most of us now understood. This was a God who cared very deeply. For many years, Noah had tried to teach us; he had tried to warn us. Each time, he had given us an opportunity to be saved—no, not just to be saved but to save ourselves from this destruction. The ark was just the vehicle by which we could be lifted above these waters. Our faith and belief in God's word, which Noah had taught, and our willingness to obey that word and to take action on it would have been what allowed God to save us in that ark.

I know not who will read these words. Perhaps it will be you, Noah. If so, I know you will draw no satisfaction from being proven right. You knew that all along anyway. I know you will feel sorrow for us. But remember, you did what you could. Ultimately, the choice to ignore the word was ours. Enjoy the new world that I am sure God will provide for you.

But if you are one of Noah's children or his children's children's children, I wonder: Has the faith and strength of Noah continued to your day, or has the story of this world's cleansing lost its power, as it has been passed from generation to generation? Do you do as we did? Do you ignore the pleadings of His word? Do you grow angry at the thought of giving up pleasures of your world to obey God? I pray—I pray to the only God—that this is not the case.

Whoever you are, heed this, my final word: do not doubt the power of God. Do not doubt His grace, love, and care. All are bigger than you could possibly imagine. It was the only hope we had, and now we have no hope at all.

10

Leah's Legacy

Hope rises up on gentle wings of hearts' desires and wistful dreams.

She soars so high it sometimes seems just fueled by wild imaginings.

—"Hope Rises Up"

For I know the plans I have for you, declares the Lord, plans for welfare and not for evil, to give you a future and a hope.

—Jeremiah 29:11 (NKJV)

Hopelessness has surprised me with patience.

—Margaret Wheatley

In 1990, the Atlanta Braves signed Rafael Belliard, a free agent shortstop, to a Major League contract. The signing didn't make much of a ripple in the sports news for that day—or for any day after that. After all, the Braves were coming off a dismal season that featured ninety-seven losses and a sixth-place finish in the National League West. Belliard was a good player, but he had been used only sparingly by his former team, the Pirates. But Braves management saw something there, and the diminutive Dominican became a stalwart of the Braves infield for the next few years. He was part of the team that eventually won fourteen straight division titles. Raffy, as he was sometimes called, was not the star hitter for the Braves, but he wasn't hired for that. He was hired for his defense, and he did an excellent job as he compiled a .984 cumulative fielding average in eight seasons for the Braves.

All ballplayers want to hit. Unfortunately, Belliard's batting average didn't quite match his defense as he compiled a .223 average with Atlanta. The story I heard was that one day, after yet another weak ground-out, Belliard came into the dugout, jammed his bat back into the bat rack, looked at manager Bobby Cox, and, in his Dominican-tinged English, said, "I hopeless." However, just a few years later, toward the end of his career, Raffy hit a line drive home run into the left field stands at Shea Stadium. It was his second Major League home run, coming ten years after the first one. He had been telling everyone who would listen that before his playing days were over, he wanted to hit just one more homer, and despite his comment to Cox, he never gave up hope.

Baseball, of course, is not the only life activity where people sometimes feel hopeless. There aren't too many of us who haven't, at one time or another, looked at a situation or a task and muttered those words: "This is hopeless." It might have been a project with a tight deadline, traffic on the way to work, a situation with a fellow employee, or a relationship with a family member. It might have even been after a doctor said something like, "We're going to have to go in another direction on this treatment."

"This is hopeless."

But really, things never are totally hopeless, especially to those who are in Christ. "Now may the God of hope fill you with all joy and peace in believing, that you may abound in hope by the power of the Holy Spirit" (Romans 15:13 NKJV).

Now, I could list a lot of scriptures about hope, but reading about it doesn't make it suddenly appear in your life. You might really believe all of those words, but still there's that nagging doubt. You look at your situation and wonder how in the world it can improve, which chases any hope out the door. You're not alone, of course. I've been there, buried in self-doubt and self-loathing, worried about what was going to happen next, seeing no way out of the situation, and seeing no way that anything was going to improve. I've hurt people, driven wedges between me and others, and have boxed myself into corners. I've lifted my eyes heavenward and said, "I hopeless."

I can recall someone in scripture who felt that way—Judas. Here was an obviously well-educated man, the keeper of the treasury for Jesus and the other disciples. But more than that, he was one of the apostles, close to Jesus every day. Judas heard the teachings and saw the miracles. He was one of the seventy who Jesus sent on a mission trip. It's safe to assume that Judas may have performed some miracles, as the disciples came back saying they had done so. Yet for some reason, Judas decided to betray Jesus for thirty pieces of silver. We don't know why because we're never told why. But the lesson of Judas isn't why he betrayed Jesus; it's how he reacted, once he realized his error.

This man, now contrite and ashamed, tried to give back the money, perhaps thinking that if he did so, the crucifixion might be stopped. But the die was cast. The priests who had paid him refused to take the blood money back, so Judas cast it on the floor in front of them. Then he went and hanged himself.

Imagine, for a moment, the hopelessness that must have filled the heart of Judas. He knew Jesus was innocent, and he knew he was responsible for the death of this innocent man. I'm sure that he could imagine the hatred that would be rained upon him for his act, and it was just too much for him to bear.

But it was not hopeless. Imagine, now, if Judas had made a more substantial repentance and had not just tried to give the money back but had fallen to his hands and knees and begged forgiveness from the Father. It's hard for us to comprehend, but based on Jesus's own words, forgiveness was available to Judas. How many times had the Savior forgiven someone who, it appears, didn't even ask? Yes, Jesus's compassion would have extended to the very one who had betrayed Him to be crucified on a cross. How do I know? I know because of eleven words uttered by Jesus on that cross: "Father, forgive them, for they do not know what they do" (Luke 23:34 NKJV).

Sadly, Judas didn't hear those words. Despite all the teachings from

Jesus about God's love and forgiveness that he'd heard over the past three years, and despite the examples of the Savior's compassion to the darkest of sinners, Judas chose to say, "I hopeless," as he swung at the end of a rope. He is a reminder for us all that it doesn't matter how close you are to Jesus; you can still be far from His heart.

Maybe this is you. Maybe you're thinking that right now. "You just don't know what I've done. You just don't know who I am. You just don't know." No, I don't know. But I know there's a Savior who loves you and wants you to understand that it's not hopeless. So I'm not going to concentrate on hopelessness in this chapter; I'm concentrating on hope. There's a great example of hope in the person of one woman who, at first glance, seemed to be in a most hopeless situation, one in which no one would blame her for just giving up. But she didn't. Let's talk about her legacy—the legacy of Leah.

The Backstory

The beginning of Leah's story can be found in Genesis 29. But before we go there, we should cover a little more of the backstory. Parts of it are important to the story.

A man named Isaac and his wife, Rebekah, had twin sons, Jacob and Esau. Because he'd been born just a few minutes ahead of his brother, Esau was the oldest and was the recipient of a birthright, which in that culture allowed him to inherit his father's estate and become head of the household upon Isaac's death. At least, that's the way it usually worked.

Esau was Isaac's favorite; you know how dads are with the oldest. Rebekah doted on Jacob, maybe because he was the baby or maybe because he was more of a homebody, sticking to the tents. Esau was a man of action; he's called a "cunning hunter," we're told, in the King James Version.

Apparently, he wasn't quite as cunning as he thought. One day, he came in from the fields, tired and hungry after a hard day's work. Jacob had some red stew cooking on the stove, and it smelled so good Esau could hardly wait to taste it. "Please give me some of that stew," he said to Jacob. "I'm so tired."

Jacob sensed an opportunity. "Sell me your birthright today," he told Esau.

"Look, I'm about to die here; what's a birthright to me?" Esau answered.

Now, when my middle daughter was very young and hunger struck, she would tell us, "I'm starving for death!" That's basically what Esau was saying. Obviously, he wasn't going to die if he didn't get that stew, but it smelled and looked so good. (Note to self: Good illustration for a future sermon on temptation.) So Esau sold his birthright for a bowl of stew. I hope it was as tasty as he imagined.

Let's fast-forward a few years. Isaac was on his deathbed, with his sight failing. He called for Esau and asked him to go out and hunt some fresh game, then prepare it for what would possibly be a last meal. With that meal, Isaac would give Esau his blessing. Esau did as he was ordered. Unfortunately, Rebekah was within earshot. She wanted her favorite son to get the blessing, and she hatched a plot to fool Isaac. It worked like a charm. A choice goat from the flock, his mother's cooking, his brother's clothes, some goat skin on his hands and neck, and some heavy-duty lying secured Isaac's blessing for Jacob.

It was about this time that Esau came home with his kill for the day. He carefully prepared the meat and expectantly presented it to his father.

"Who are you?" Isaac asked.

"I'm Esau, your firstborn," Esau answered.

When Isaac realized what had happened, the only thing he could do was give Esau another blessing, one not quite as choice as the one given to Jacob, especially the line that said, "You shall serve your brother."

Esau's hatred welled up inside. "When the days of mourning for my father are done, then I will kill my brother Jacob," he vowed to himself. Somehow, Rebekah heard about his anger and decided it might be wise to send Jacob away while Esau cooled off. The plan was to send him to her brother Laban's place in Haran for a few days. She convinced Isaac that she was afraid Jacob might find an attractive woman to marry among the local Canaanite women. Isaac, not wanting this to happen, told Jacob to go to Laban's house to find a wife among his own people.

When Esau heard about all this, he decided to do something to spite Isaac and Rebekah. His father didn't want Jacob marrying one of the locals, a Canaanite woman. So to get back for the slight, Esau went to Ishmael, Isaac's half-brother, and found a woman named Mahalath to take as a wife.

While Jacob was traveling to his uncle's place, he stopped along the way to rest and had the well-known "Jacob's ladder" dream. In this dream, God promised the blessings of Jacob's grandfather, Abraham, to Esau. "Your descendants shall be as the dust of the earth … and in you and in your seed, all the families of the earth shall be blessed," God said (Genesis 28:14 NKJV). When he awoke, Jacob was amazed by the dream. He declared, "How awesome is this place! This is none other than the house of God, and this is the gate of heaven!" (Genesis 28:17 NKJV).

Because of this dream, Jacob's attitude and focus changed. He had received the blessing of his earthly father, Isaac, and now, in this dream, he had been blessed by his heavenly Father. He took the stone he'd used as a pillow and set it up as an altar, pouring oil on it. Then, he gave the place a name—Bethel, House of God. After he finished these acts, he made a vow: "If God will be with me, and keep me in this way that I am going, and give me bread to eat and clothing to put on, so that I come back to my father's house in peace, then the LORD shall be my God. And this stone which I have set as a pillar shall be God's house, and of all that You give me I will surely give a tenth to You" (Genesis 28:20–22 NKJV).

His hope, his prayer, is that when he does return, there will be peace. His commitment to this peace and to giving to God will be tested much sooner than he suspects.

Jacob leaves Bethel and continues his journey to Laban's. He soon arrives at a well, where some of Laban's friends are gathered, waiting for all the flocks to gather to roll the stone from the well and water the sheep. As Jacob talks with the men, Laban's daughter, Rachel, brings her sheep to the well. Jacob is immediately smitten. He rolls the stone away so Rachel can water her sheep. Then he kisses her, lifts up his voice, and weeps. It is a romantic moment.

Rachel runs to tell her father about Jacob. When Laban hears that his nephew is in town, he runs to meet him, embraces him, and brings him home. Jacob stays for a month, obviously helping on the farm. Laban finally says, "Because you are my relative, should you therefore serve me for nothing? Tell me, what should your wages be?" (Genesis 29:15 NKJV).

Jacob is head over heels in love with Rachel. "I'll work for you seven years if you'll give me Rachel, your younger daughter, as my wife." Laban agrees to the deal. "So Jacob served seven years for Rachel, and they seemed only a few days to him because of the love he had for her" (Genesis 29:20 NKJV).

At the end of the seven years, Jacob demands his payment—Rachel. Laban throws a big wedding feast, inviting everyone in town. But that night, in the darkness, he pulls a switch on Jacob. Instead of bringing Rachel to him, he brings his oldest daughter, Leah. Somehow, Jacob doesn't discover what has happened until morning. It must have been a rude awakening, to say the least.

Jacob is furious. "'What is this you have done to me? Was it not for Rachel that I served you? Why then have you deceived me?' And Laban said, 'It must not be done so in our country, to give the younger before the firstborn'" (Genesis 29:25–26 NKJV).

Today, whenever you install a computer program or purchase a car, you'll see a lot of "Terms and Conditions" in the contract. It's that fine print we all ignore. Apparently, there was some fine print that Jacob did not take the time to read.

As a side note, I wonder how long it took for Jacob to hearken back to his deceit in stealing his father's blessing from Esau? There was Isaac, blind and in the dark, just as Jacob was in the dark on his wedding night.

Laban tells Jacob to wait a week, perhaps until all the wedding guests have gone home and can't take back the gifts. At that time, he will give Rachel to Jacob—in exchange for another seven years of work. Jacob agrees to the deal.

Leah's Story

Now comes Leah's story, which, given the circumstances, seems somewhat sad. But maybe all is not as it seems.

The account in Genesis 29:17 tells us that Leah's eyes were delicate, but Rachel was beautiful of form and appearance. This is from the New King James translation. Other translations say Leah's eyes were weak, tender, or soft. Much debate has gone on over the years as to what this means. Were her eyes tender? Did she have doe eyes? Were her eyes weary? When I read this, I can't help but notice that the scriptures only talk about Leah's eyes while they mention how beautiful in every way Rachel was. This is the Old Testament equivalent of, "She has a nice personality."

According to *Strong's Concordance*, in Hebrew, the name *Leah* means "to be weary, to be impatient, to be grieved, to be offended." It wasn't until Jacob showed up that the name really began to fit the woman. Imagine, for a moment, how you would feel, given the situation.

I wonder what it must have been like for Leah, the oldest, to see a really good prospect come along, only to fall for her younger sister. Was she offended? Was she grieved? Now, it may have seemed natural to Leah that this man would fall for Rachel, and it may not have bothered her at all. After all, it's apparent from what we read that she wasn't quite as pretty as her sister. Who knows if other suitors had come along and been rejected? Seven years of interaction between the sisters and Jacob go by in just a couple of verses.

About those seven years: what must it have felt like for Leah to watch Jacob work every day on her father's farm—for Rachel's hand? Leah knew the customs of the country as well as anyone; she may well have felt some of that impatience during those years, longing for someone to come and sweep her off her feet, to come and show her the same love and devotion as Jacob showed for Rachel. But at the end of those seven years, he had not come. There was no one for her, and she knew Rachel was going to have Jacob, against the customs of her land. Toward the end, the weariness of waiting may have begun to weigh on her heart.

But then, her father came to her with a crazy scheme. The night of the wedding, Laban went to fetch Jacob's bride and bring her to him (while Jacob probably waited impatiently!). However, instead of going to Rachel's room, he went to Leah's, and he brought her to Jacob. As far as we know, Leah didn't ask for this; it was all her father's doing. Whether it was deceit from the very beginning or something Laban came up with at the last minute, it was not Leah's plan. Of course, she did go along with it.

What must have gone through her mind that wedding night (other than not speaking)? Perhaps she thought Jacob would understand and accept her father's substitution. Again, we don't know what type of relationship Jacob and Leah had during those seven years. It was probably at least a cordial one. To use another cliché, he may have "loved her like a sister."

Maybe, as Leah silently slipped into the room and into Jacob's waiting arms, her thought was, *When he finds out it's me, he'll love me.* But that was not to be because even though Jacob accepted his new, unwanted bride, and even though he fulfilled the week with Leah, after that week was up, he turned to Rachel. "Jacob also went in to Rachel, and he also loved Rachel more than Leah" (Genesis 29:30 NKJV).

Jacob loved Rachel more. But Leah's plight was noticed by the one who mattered. "When the LORD saw that Leah was unloved, He opened her womb; but Rachel was barren" (Genesis. 29:31NKJV).

The Hebrew word for "unloved" in this passage is *sane*, and in all the lexicons and commentaries I've checked, it means exactly what you think it does—to be hated. The word refers to an emotional hatred, as with an enemy. It's used in Genesis 37:8, when we're told that Joseph's brothers hated him even more for his dreams and words; in Leviticus 19:17, when God says, "You shall not hate your brother"; and in over 140 other Old Testament passages. Jacob didn't just dislike Leah; he hated her.

Some of that may well have been transference—the hatred of his situation and of Laban's deceit raining down on Leah. We've all been guilty of the same attitude. How many times have we let our frustrations and anger spill over to others who just happened to be handy? A job is lost, and suddenly you begin to think your once-loving family is against you, causing your relationship with them to take a huge hit. You don't really hate them; you hate what's happened and really believe they may have been part of it.

So Jacob spent that week with Leah, performing the husbandly duties for her, while wishing all the time that it was Rachel and while seething with anger at Laban's cruel trick. Resentment must have roiled inside of him, until at last he could have the woman of his dreams. Yes, Leah was hated. At some point Leah must have uttered those sad words, "This is hopeless."

When the Lord saw that Leah was hated, He opened her womb. This small blessing from God led to a legacy of hope for her sons, her grandchildren, her many ancestors, and for all of us.

Leah's Legacy of Hope

Imagine the bittersweet joy when Leah discovered she was pregnant with her first child. Jacob came in from a hard day of work to find her staring at him with a slight smile on her face. "I am with child," she might have told him. After a few seconds of thought, he may have had a slight smile of his own; he may have kissed her on the cheek and squeezed her hand—before running to tell Rachel.

But Leah wasn't bitter, at least not toward God. When her child was born, it was a son, and the scripture tells us she named him Reuben, which means "behold, a son." It was just about the best gift any wife could give her husband—a son as the firstborn—and the Lord had given her this gift to present to Jacob. "The LORD has surely looked on my affliction," she said, "now therefore, my husband will love me."

Apparently, it didn't work as well as she wished because when she had another son, she named him Simeon, which means "heard." Maybe Jacob's ears were closed, but God was listening. "Because the LORD has heard that I am unloved, He has therefore given me this son also," she reasoned. But again, Jacob stubbornly maintained that emotional distance from Leah.

According to the scripture, she became pregnant a third time and gave Jacob a third son, whom she named Levi, which means "attached." As before, she hopefully reasoned, "Now this time, my husband will become attached to me, because I have borne him three sons." Nope. She conceived and bore Jacob yet another son. This time, she turned to the one she knew beyond doubt loved her. Leah named her fourth son Judah, which means "praise."

"Now I will praise the LORD," she said after the birth.

There are a couple of points that we need to unpack right here. First of all, despite the fact that he hated Leah, Jacob obviously fulfilled his husbandly duties. Can we say he was just being a man, doing what guys do? That might be the first thought that comes to mind, but consider that there was another woman in the household, one whom he desired and loved more than Leah. You could make the case that Reuben was conceived during that week of fulfillment after the wedding ceremony and before Rachel was available. But how do you explain the other three sons? Could it be that the anger and hatred began to subside at some point? All you have to do is go back to verse 30 and reread what it says: Then Jacob also went in to Rachel, and he also loved Rachel more than Leah. Jacob loved Rachel *more* than he loved Leah. That means he did love her, at least a little. It's like when someone says, "I could care less." We grammar Nazis know that's incorrect and bristle at the use of that phrase. "I guess you do care, at least a little," is what we say.

Now, to be accurate, the word *more* isn't in the original Hebrew. It was added by interpreters, much, much later. But as the story of Jacob and Leah unfolds, putting that word in the text makes perfect sense. Yes, he hated her in the beginning, but I believe the hatred softened to at least an approximation of love—or at least an appreciation.

The second point deals with one aspect of Leah's legacy. Go back and reread Genesis 29:32–35. If you look closely, you'll see someone stronger and more faithful than you may have imagined. With each successive son, she still hoped to gain or earn Jacob's love.

Leah never lost hope.

Like Rafael Belliard, "It's hopeless" is what she could have said, given the situation, given the hatred. But despite everything, she continued to place her hope in God. She knew God heard her and loved her. She hoped Jacob would change his heart and love her—just a little. I wonder if God's gift of sons was at least partially a reward for her hopefulness.

Hopelessness is what we all sometimes feel. We're lonely, afflicted by the attitudes and emotions of others. We feel unloved. Maybe we've gotten the diagnosis, and we're told by the doctor there's nothing he can do; it's too late. Or maybe we lose a son or daughter to death or to wandering away into a life of godlessness. I've been there. Yet I know it's not hopeless. I know just as much and as surely as Leah knew that there's a God in heaven who looks down on me and encircles me with His love. It may take me a while to realize it, or it may take a two-by-four upside the head to bring me to my senses, but I get there.

When I get in a situation such as that, I often think of a scene from one of my favorite movies, *Call Northside 777*. Based on a true story, the movie stars Jimmy Stewart as a hard-boiled reporter who begins a human-interest story about a mother who posted an ad in the newspaper. Her son is in prison for life after being convicted of killing a policeman in Prohibition-era Chicago. He has always maintained his innocence, and his mother has been scrubbing floors and working other jobs for ten years, trying to scrape together enough money to offer a reward, in the hope that someone will provide new information that can clear her son. The reporter is not convinced in the beginning, but later, he begins to realize that the man is innocent. Toward the end, the paper decides to pull out of the case to keep the son from jeopardizing a possible future parole. The reporter visits the mother to break the bad news. As he's leaving, the mother, a Polish immigrant, says, "If you go, who's gonna help me? I got no friends." After the reporter leaves, she leans against a bureau next to a wall, softly crying. After a moment, she looks up to see a large crucifix hanging on the wall. "Big fool, me," she says as a smile comes across her face. "I got a friend."

Yes, we all "got a friend", someone who loves us and comforts us in our hopelessness, someone who assures us that there's hope in any situation if we'll just cling to Him, lean on Him, and hope in Him.

Leah's Legacy of Faithfulness

There's one other aspect of Leah's legacy that we need to consider—her faithfulness. It filtered down to some very unlikely recipients.

As the narrative goes along, Rachel becomes upset because she's lagging so far behind in the son sweepstakes. So, after much nagging of her husband, she gives her handmaid to Jacob. This, of course, was a common practice in those days. It wasn't always the best thing to do—see the story of Abraham, Sarah, and Hagar for full details. But in this case, things seem to go fairly well, as two sons are born of Rachel's handmaid, Bilhah. Leah continues to try to earn Jacob's love by giving her handmaid, Zilpah, to Jacob. Two more sons are born! Much later, the psalmist would say, "Like arrows in the hand of a warrior, so are the children of one's youth. Happy is the man who has his quiver full of them." Jacob's quiver is overflowing, but it isn't over yet.

Not long after the birth of the eighth son, Leah's firstborn, Reuben, is out working in the fields and finds some mandrakes. Being a nice son, he brings them home to his mother because they could possibly be quite useful. You see, the Hebrew for *mandrakes* is loosely translated as "the love apple." In that day and time, pagans used the plant in some of their rituals, and some still do to this day. *Harry Potter* fans may recognize the name from some of those novels. But over and above the rituals, the mandrake was thought to increase fertility.

You can understand why Rachel becomes very interested when she sees them; after all, she is still barren and, understandably, anxious to give her husband a son or two on her own. By the way, don't think her spoiled or nefarious; remember that she is the one Jacob wanted from the beginning. She loved the man and wanted to make him happy. So she asks Leah to share some of those "love apples" with her. Leah is willing, but only if Rachel is willing to let her sleep with Jacob that night.

Doesn't this episode seem very similar to another incident in Jacob's life? That first time, Esau came in from the fields and was so hungry he thought he would die, so he agreed to sell his birthright. This time, Rachel is so desperate and so hungry to give Jacob a son that she agreed to give her husband, the love of her life, to her sister for the night. But instead of the plan working for Rachel, Leah ends up conceiving two more times.

What a contrast we have in this situation. On the one hand, there's Rachel, loved so much by Jacob, desperately trying to give her husband a son. On the other hand, there's Leah, desperately trying to earn Jacob's love by giving him son after son after son. She even names her sixth son Zebulun, which means "dwelling," in the hope that, perhaps now, Jacob will find a dwelling place for her in his heart.

But you see, Leah could never earn Jacob's love, and Rachel could not force Jacob to care more. This is similar to the way many people today try to earn the love of God. Can I give more of my income, more of my time? Do I show up for worship every time the doors are open, go on a mission trip, or spend five hours a day studying His word? How can I make Him love me?

You can't. He already loves you, more than you can imagine. You are the apple of His eye. He cares so much for you that He was willing to give His Son. There is nothing you can do to make Him love you more. All He asks is your faithfulness and your trust in His guidance—the same type of faithfulness and trust that guided Leah's hope.

Leah's Legacy to Her Children and Beyond

If you want to see the immediate effects of Leah's legacy of hopefulness and faithfulness, look no further than her children. Yes, they had their problems, issues, and failings, but their mother taught them some valuable lessons as well.

When God finally opened Rachel's womb and allowed her to give Jacob a son, Joseph, Jacob loved him more. It's no surprise Jacob would love Joseph more; he was just taking after his own father and mother. This favoritism made all the other sons jealous and resentful; they hated Joseph. All eleven of them, by the way. That includes not just Leah's sons but the ones from Zilpah and Bilhah. This led the brothers to plot how they could kill the boy, who had those crazy dreams about them bowing down to him. But Reuben would not go along with the plan. "Cast him into the pit," he told them, "but don't hurt him." His intention was to come back to the pit, pull Joseph out, and "bring him back to his father." He saw Joseph in his affliction and, though he probably hated him as much as his brothers, he could not bring himself to kill the dreamer.

There are two points to consider. First, it's easy to imagine Reuben sitting at the feet of his mother, Leah, listening to her tell how God had been so kind to her and how much she depended on Him. This may have been what softened his heart when Joseph's life was in jeopardy. This word *hate* used here is the same one used earlier to describe Jacob's feelings toward Leah. As the oldest, Reuben had observed not only his mother's attitude but his father's as well. Despite the seeming hatred for Leah, there was a place for her in Jacob's heart. As Reuben observed Joseph coming toward him and his brothers and as he heard their plotting, some semblance of tenderness must have gone through his mind. Somehow, he couldn't bring himself to hate Joseph that much. Of course, this is conjecture, not scripture. Remember, while it's true that Reuben, son of the unloved Leah, helped save Joseph's life by his actions, it's also true that later, he lay with Rachel's handmaid, Bilhah.

The second important point to consider is that it was from the tribe of Judah that Jesus came. Jesus was a direct descendant not of Joseph or Benjamin, Rachel's sons, but of Judah, the fourth son of Leah, the unloved. Yes, God worked through Joseph to get them to Egypt and back to the Promised Land. But He also worked through Judah to get us all to the real Promised Land.

Let's think about that story of Rachel's son Joseph for just a moment. Isn't it interesting that he was sold into slavery and eventually rose to second in command of Potiphar's house, second in command of the prison, and second in command of Egypt? I wonder where he learned to be satisfied with second place, where he learned to hope in the Lord and to trust in His grace, mercy, and love.

Rachel struggled so to give her husband sons, but in the end, the cost was her life. She died in childbirth and was buried beside the road leading to Bethlehem. Some years later, Leah died. She was placed in the tomb with some other famous couples—Abraham and Sarah, and

Isaac and Rebekah—in the tomb where Jacob himself was eventually laid to rest. Leah, the unloved, had finally found the special place in Jacob's heart for which she had her hoped.

When you look at the story of Leah, it's easy to come away thinking that it was hopeless, that no one would blame her if she said, like Rafael Belliard, "I hopeless." It's a story filled with unrequited love, with someone knowing she held no better than second place in someone's heart. It's the story of a woman begging for the affection of her husband. But there's so much more there. J. M. Barrie, the author of *Peter Pan*, said this: "Let no one who loves be called altogether unhappy. Even love unreturned has its rainbow."

Leah's rainbow was the love of her heavenly Father. She may have been second in Jacob's heart, but she knew she was first in God's. Her battle cry was, "Never give up, keep plugging away against the odds, have faith in God and hope in His plan."

In Ruth 4, when the people were celebrating the coming marriage of Ruth and Boaz, this is what they said: "And all the people who were at the gate, and the elders, said, 'We are witnesses. The LORD make the woman who is coming to your house like Rachel and Leah, the two who built the house of Israel; and may you prosper in Ephrathah and be famous in Bethlehem'" (Ruth 4:11 NKJV).

Leah turned a seemingly hopeless situation into a monumental and memorable life, one that people generations later were extoling in song. Her love for her husband and her love for her sons cannot be doubted. But more important, her love for God shines brightly through the story of her life. Leah's hope rose on those gentle wings and reached to her heavenly Father with a prayer for her heart's desire. She joined her love and faithfulness with an abundance of hope to leave us a lasting and wonderful legacy.

"I hopeless"? No, not in God's plans.

11

Hope

Hope's song is sweet and crystal clear, and if we take the time to hear,

It calms the heart all filled with fear and guides us home when night is near.

—"Hope Rises Up"

Return to the stronghold, you prisoners of hope. Even today I declare that I will restore double to you.

—Zechariah 9:12

We have always held to the hope, the belief, the conviction that there is a better life, a better world, beyond the horizon.

—Franklin D. Roosevelt

As I began work on this chapter, someone posted the following quote on my Facebook page: "Every night we go to bed without the assurance of being alive the next morning, but we set the alarm anyway. That's called hope." It's as good a definition of hope as any and seems rather appropriate to use at this point. We talked about hopelessness and Leah's hope in the last chapter, but just what is hope?

There are lots of definitions for hope. Wikipedia, the fount of all knowledge, gives us this statement: "Hope is an optimistic state of mind that is based on an expectation of positive outcomes with respect to events and circumstances in one's life or the world at large. As a verb, its definitions include: 'expect with confidence' and 'to cherish a desire with anticipation.' Among its opposites are dejection, hopelessness, and despair."

Emily Dickinson was a little more poetic in her observation, as you might expect: "Hope is the thing with feathers that perches in the soul and sings the tune without the words and never stops at all."

Hope is a universal theme running through literature, movies, TV, and music. When the original *Star Wars* was renamed, George Lucas chose to call it *A New Hope* because it looked forward to something better. Lee Ann Womack sings "I Hope You Dance," encouraging listeners to never give up (obviously, she's never seen me dance). The TV show *Saving Hope* dealt with doctors and nurses trying to keep hope alive at the aptly named Hope Zion Hospital. The four young ladies held captive for ten years in a Cleveland house titled their memoir, *Hope—A Memoir of Survival in Cleveland*. For those ladies, hope of rescue, hope of escape, or any hope at all was what kept them alive through all those dark years. Sometimes, hope is all there is in life.

But hope is another of those words that has lost its impact through the years. Think about how often you use *hope* in your day-to-day life. "I hope I make that green light!" "I hope they have roasted vegetables in the cafeteria today." "I hope I make it home before my favorite TV show comes on." That kind of hope doesn't quite carry the same weight as the hope of a young lady who has been kept prisoner for ten years or the hopeful statements made by a frightened husband in a hospital waiting room, thinking about his wife in surgery.

I looked on dictionary.com to find out where this word came from. The word is Middle English and dates from somewhere before 900. It's derived from the Old English word *hopa*, and it has some Dutch and German roots.

I thought it was rather poetic that the section for the derivation of the word was titled, "Origin of Hope." As Christians, we know where the origin of hope really is—Jesus. To the Christian, hope is paramount. Hope is bound together with faith and love as one of the three main virtues of life. As Paul tells us, the greatest of these is love because when we leave this place, faith and hope will no longer be needed; we will swim in seas of love for eternity. However, here on earth, hope is sometimes the only thing keeping us from going under the waves of doubt. I have faith, yet I hope my faith is strong enough to last. I have love, yet I hope my love is deep enough to win out over my pride and prejudice. It's quite a balancing act.

The word *hope* is sprinkled throughout the scriptures, appearing in more than 150 verses, depending on the translation. Surprisingly, at least to me, the word doesn't appear until the book of Ruth, in chapter one, verse 12. A woman named Naomi and her husband had journeyed to Moab during a famine and ended up settling there. Their two sons married Moabite women, Orpah and Ruth. In the course of time, the husband and both sons died, leaving the three women with only each other. Naomi decided to return to Judah and the two daughters-in-law followed. Eventually, she told them to return to their own homes, but they initially refused. Finally, she reasoned with them. "Turn back, my daughters, go—for I am too old to have a husband. If I should say I have hope, *if* I should have a husband tonight and should also bear sons, would you wait for them till they were grown?" She was saying that she had no hope of having more children, and there was no hope of Orpah and Ruth getting husbands from her.

The Hebrew word used in this and other Old Testament passages is *tiqvah*. According to *Strong's Concordance*, the word is used the vast majority of times in the context of expectation. However, there is another meaning for *tiqvah*.

In Joshua 2, the spies had scoped out Jericho and the surrounding area. They ended up at the house of Rahab, a lady of means, which were made by a certain salacious activity. She was a harlot, a prostitute; she was not the most desirable of people in most circles. Someone alerted the king of the city to their presence, so he sent a message to Rahab, asking her to hand them over. She hid the spies and told the king that they'd left the city just before the gates were shut. "Pursue them quickly, for you may overtake them," she told the king. After the posse left, she made a deal with the spies. She told them she knew that their God was *the* God. She'd heard all about what He had done for His people since their release from Egypt, and she was scared. "Now therefore, I beg you, swear to me by the Lord since I have shown you kindness, that you also will show kindness to my father's house, and give me a true token, and spare my father, my mother, my brothers, my sisters, and all that they have, and deliver our lives from death" (Joshua 2:12–13 NKJV).

You remember the answer: "We will be blameless of this oath of yours which you have made us swear, unless, when we come into the land, you bind this line of scarlet cord in the window through which you let us down, and unless you bring your father, your mother, your brothers, and all your father's household to your own home" (Joshua 2:17–18 NKJV).

Three verses later, Rahab reacted: "Then she said, 'According to your words, so be it.' And she sent them away, and they departed. And she bound the scarlet cord in the window" (Joshua 2:21 NKJV).

The word used for *cord* is—you guessed it—tiqvah. Rahab, prostitute and citizen of the land God's people were about to attack (and conquer), had faith in the stories she had heard about this God. She loved her family. She tied her life to the promise of deliverance that was attached to the other end of the red tiqvah hanging out her window. The promise was her hope; the cord was a symbol of that hope.

In the other Old Testament instances where the word is translated as *hope*, the definition of expectation is very clear, but it's a rather one-sided usage. In almost all these passages, the context is man's hope for blessings from the Lord.

"You are my hiding place and my shield; I hope in Your word. Depart from me, you evildoers, for I will keep the commandments of my God! Uphold me according to Your word, that I may live; and do not let me be ashamed of my hope" (Psalm 119:114–116 NKJV).

"And I will wait on the LORD, Who hides His face from the house of Jacob; and I will hope in Him" (Isaiah 8:17 NKJV).

"For I know the thoughts that I think toward you, says the LORD, thoughts of peace and not of evil, to give you a future and a hope" (Jeremiah 29:11 NKJV).

"'The LORD is my portion,' says my soul, 'therefore I hope in Him!'" (Lamentations 3:24 NKJV).

As you might expect, there is a certain looking forward in the statements. Whatever the situation, the Lord will help, and He will provide. He will take care of the situation for the person.

In the New Testament, the writers use the Greek word *elpis*. While it does carry the thought of expectation of good, according to *Strong's Concordance*, the emphasis in most cases changes to "a joyful and confident expectation of salvation."

"And rejoice in the hope of the glory of God," Paul tells us in Romans. "There is one body and one Spirit, just as you were called in one hope of your calling," he says in Ephesians.

"Rest your hope fully upon the grace that is to be brought to you at the revelation of Jesus Christ," Peter writes.

"Everyone who has this hope in Him purifies himself," says John.

Surprisingly, the only time Jesus ever mentions the word *hope* is when He uses it in the context of our hoping for gain when we help someone, and He tells us not to have that kind of hope.

It should be obvious to even the most casual observer that the emphasis of hope in the scriptures is not hope for earthly gain. There's nothing wrong with earthly gain; it has its place and is important when we need to pay the electric bill or buy food. But pinning our hopes to earthly gain is fruitless in the end because some day it all will be gone. "The grass withers, the flower fades," Isaiah tells us.

No, the hope that the scriptures tell us about is a hope for something beyond all this, a hope to be with God, both here in this life and in eternity. It is this type of hope that can drive us through our days and sustain us through those times when the darkness closes in, and we are fearful of pain, death, or the consequences of our actions. It's also an expectation of the blessings, strength, mercy, and love that come from being a part of His kingdom.

Let's go back to the Old Testament for an example. Listen to what David had to say about the subject of hope in Psalm 16:9: "Therefore my heart is glad, and my glory rejoices; my flesh also will rest in hope" (NKJV).

Basically, David is talking about those three human entities we all talk about: heart, body, and soul. Because of the love of the Lord, the heart—our emotional side—is happy. Meanwhile, the soul—our spiritual body—rejoices in the knowledge of God's blessings and in His salvation. The flesh? Well, the flesh (or the body) can rest in the hope of eternal rest to come.

But in order to have the hope revealed, David states there must also be movement on our part. As I've said before, that's what the *therefore* is there for. This thought begins back in verse 7, where David tells us that while he's thankful for the blessings of the Lord, he's also just as thankful for the Lord's counsel—His instruction. Let's put this whole passage together, and put hope in its context.

> I will bless the LORD who has given me counsel; my heart also instructs me in the night seasons. I have set the LORD always before me; because He is at my right hand I shall not be moved. Therefore my heart is glad, and my glory rejoices; my flesh also will rest in hope. For You will not leave my soul in Sheol, nor will You allow Your Holy One to see corruption. You will show me the path of life; in Your presence is fullness of joy; at Your right hand are pleasures forevermore. (Psalm 19:7–11 NKJV)

When you read the King James Version, the word *heart* in the seventh verse is translated as *reins*—"my reins also instruct me in the night seasons." The Hebrew word used here is *kilyah*, which has two meanings: reins, such as the reins of a horse, and kidneys. Taken in the context of reins, it's easy to see David knows that the instruction of God puts reins on him and, by extension, anyone who follows the teachings and guidance of God. That makes sense when you think about it. Reins guide an animal. If you pull them to the right, the horse goes right and misses that rattlesnake in the trail. If you pull them to the left, the horse goes left and misses the gully by the side of the road. If you pull them tight, the horse stops before you both go over the cliff. God's word instructs and guides us. Guidance, of course, is essential, and it's good for God to guide us.

But there's also that other meaning, kidneys. Back in those days, people believed that the kidneys were the seat of feeling and emotions, not the heart. Used in the sense David does here, it means the will and the affections. David is saying that his will (that which now bends to God) and his affection (his love for the Lord) now "rein" him in and keep him on the right path. God's will and God's affection keep David headed toward his hope.

Sometimes, we hope for something, and that's really all we do. In one episode of *Leave It to Beaver*, "Beaver's Library Book," Beaver borrows his dad's library card to check out *Treasure Island* for a book report. He promptly loses the book. Notices are sent to his dad, but Beaver intercepts them all as he continues to search for the book. Good old Eddie Haskell finds out about it and warns Beaver that he'd better pay the fines, or "they'll throw your old man in jail," which prompts Beaver to visit the library and beg for mercy. The librarian assures him Ward will not be sent to jail and urges him to confess to his father. When Beaver finally gets up the nerve to tell his dad what happened, Ward asks him why he didn't just say something before it all got out of hand. "I kept hopin' I'd find it," Beaver says. Ward looks him in the eyes and says, "Beaver, you can't go through life hoping for things." How true.

"I hope I get that raise," but we don't do anything worthy of a raise. "I hope I can lose weight," but we still don't eat right or exercise. Like Beaver Cleaver, our hope is built on the proverbial shifting sands; it is nothing but a figment of our imaginations.

But our spiritual hope must be deeper than that; it must be more. Listen to how Peter describes it in 1 Peter 1:3: "Blessed be the God and Father of our Lord Jesus Christ, who according to His abundant mercy has begotten us again to a living hope through the resurrection of Jesus Christ from the dead" (NKJV).

I don't think there's any doubt about his meaning. Just as our faith must be alive, so should our hope. Hope must have an effect on our actions, inside and outside the kingdom. I hope to get to heaven, but what am I doing to point myself in the right direction? I should never be ashamed to be reined in by the Lord. It's my only hope.

What else does Peter say? "Be ready always to give an answer for the hope that's within you." I should never be afraid or ashamed to let others know about this hope I have. It's their only hope too.

In Romans, Paul tells us that Abraham hoped against hope. I would imagine that there were some days that hope was all that kept him going. Hope was what gave him strength to rescue Lot. Hope was what gave him courage to bargain for Sodom and Gomorrah. Hope was what steadied his hand when he raised the knife to sacrifice Isaac. "If God wants me to sacrifice this son, who was such a long time in coming, He must have a reason," his actions said. "My hope is anchored to the promise of a great nation. I'll do what the Lord asks." In Hebrews 11, the writer tells us Abraham reasoned that if God could give him a son from what was considered by everyone to be the dead womb of Sarah, He certainly could raise Isaac from the dead. But before he could plunge the knife into his son's body, the angel of God called out to him and told him to stop. Abraham saw his hope fulfilled!

Sometimes, we see our hope fulfilled as well, in both secular and spiritual matters. For instance, those of us who are parents, like me, do a lot of hoping for our children. We hope they do well in school; we hope they make the right kinds of friends; we hope they listen to those sermons and Bible school classes; we hope they grow to be good followers of the Lord and good citizens of the land. Most of the time, we follow Peter's admonition to possess a living hope. We teach our children right from wrong and good from bad. We read the Bible stories, set good examples, and pray for them. We help with homework, support them in their activities, and encourage them to discover and develop their talents. Then one day—in the blink of an eye, it seems—they're grown, and we get to see how all that work and all that hope play out.

On the spiritual side, our hope is anchored to the promise of salvation in Christ. Because of that promise and our hope in the truth of the promise, we spend our days walking in the light as best we can. When we fail, we hope in the promise of mercy and forgiveness. As we walk the pathway of life, we exult in the hope of heaven, a home with Him beyond this land of disappointments, aches and pains, fear, anxiety, and loneliness. As Paul tells us in Romans 8:24, "We were saved in this hope."

But some days, weeks, months, or even years, the world gets to us. It often seems as if everything goes wrong, as if the weight of the world is on our shoulders. When those times come, we need to lean on that hope as much as possible, revel in the promises, and see beyond the now to what will be one day. Not everyone, however, can do that.

Mark O. Barton was born on April 2, 1955, in Stockbridge, Georgia. By most accounts, he had a fairly standard childhood, although the family did move around some because his father was in the air force. He attended college and earned a chemistry degree. Later, he married, and he and his wife had two children. Barton and his family eventually moved to Alabama for his job.

During his college days, Barton developed a drug habit, which may have led to some of the problems he was to face in later years. While in Alabama, he became paranoid and was very distrustful of his wife. During this period, he was fired from his job because his performance at work did not meet the necessary level. As a final act of revenge against his employer, he tried to sabotage company data, but he was caught and ended up spending a short time in jail. After his jail time, Barton moved the family back to Georgia, where he got a new job. Along with the job, he picked up a girlfriend, who was a friend of his wife's. In 1993, his wife and mother-in-law were murdered. As you might expect, Barton was the number-one suspect, but there was not enough evidence to charge him. He ended up marrying the girlfriend in 1995, and shortly afterward, Barton invested the nearly $300,000 insurance settlement that he'd received from his first wife's death on a new career—day trading.

Barton liked the high-risk stocks, mostly those related to the internet. By 1999, however, day trading was not working well for him. He had lost over $100,000, and one of the securities companies he frequented had canceled his account.

In the early morning hours of July 27, 1999, Mark Barton beat his wife, Leigh Ann, to death while she was sleeping in their bed. The next night, he turned his rage on his children, Matthew and Mychelle, beating them both to death, as he had their stepmother. The next day, July 29, he went to the offices of Momentum Securities in the Buckhead area of Atlanta, pulled out two pistols, and opened fire. Four people were killed there. Barton then walked to All-Tech Investment Group and again opened fire, killing another five workers, before finally making his getaway.

Four hours later, Barton attempted to kidnap a young lady in Kennesaw, a small town about twenty miles to the north. Officials believe that he may have been attempting to use her as a hostage for an escape. She was able to get away and call police. Officers chased Barton and cornered him at a gas station. It was there that Barton turned the gun on himself. Here are some of the words from the notes Barton left behind:

> I killed Leigh Ann because she was one of the main reasons for my demise ... I know that Jehovah will take care of all of them in the next life. I'm sure the details don't matter. There is no excuse, no good reason I am sure no one will understand. If they could I wouldn't want them to ... I don't plan to live very much longer, just long enough to kill as many of the people that greedily sought my destruction ... I have been dying since October. I wake up at night so afraid, so terrified, that I couldn't be that afraid while awake. It has taken its toll. I have come to hate this life and this system of things. I have come to have no hope.

How utterly heartbreaking. Twelve people killed, another thirteen wounded, and lives shattered and scarred—all because he blamed some of them for bringing that hopelessness on him. The lives of two innocent children were taken because this man couldn't bear for them to be as hopeless as he was.

You can say a lot about this episode. You can say Mark Barton was looking for earthly gain, for happiness in money or in the power that he felt when he was able to make a good score in the stock market. He hoped that he would be able to find a stock that would go up. He hoped that he would be able to make back the money that he lost. He may have even hoped to get a better house or better car, to give his wife things she wanted, or to give his children a good education—if only he could score the winning stocks he hoped for. He hoped for lots of things, but really, in the end, he had no hope because his hope was built on the wrong foundation.

Compare that story to this one:

Edward Mote was born in London in 1797 to poor, ungodly parents. In his own words, "My Sundays were spent in the streets. So ignorant was I that I did not know that there was a God." The school he attended didn't allow a Bible to be seen, much less taught. At the age of sixteen, he was apprenticed to a cabinetmaker who, as it turned out, was a believer. God does work in mysterious ways, after all. The cabinetmaker took Mote to hear a famed evangelist of the time, and the words of the evangelist piqued his curiosity. Before long, Mote was baptized and became devoted to Christ—a dedicated churchgoer. He continued as a cabinetmaker in London for over thirty years before finally deciding to enter the ministry in his fifties.

Through the years, he wrote and published more than one hundred hymns, the most well-known being "My Hope Is Built on Nothing Less," which you may know as "The Solid Rock." Mote's original hymn had six verses, but most hymnals today only include four. Here are the other two verses:

> My hope is built on nothing less than Jesus' blood and righteousness;
> 'Midst all the Hell I feel within, on His completed work I lean.
> I trust His righteous character, His council, promise, and His power;
> His honor and His name's at stake, to save me from the burning lake.[3]

---

[3] Kenneth W. Osbeck, "The Solid Rock," in *101 More Hymn Stories* (Grand Rapids, MI: Kregel Publications, 2013), 276.

Edward Mote was a child of the streets, someone well acquainted with adversity. Apparently, his parents were not overly concerned with his raising—not uncommon in England at that time. Who could blame him for being resentful? Who could blame him for scoffing at the thought of a God who loved him? Yet something drove him to that first evangelical meeting. Maybe he did it only because he hoped it would please his master. But what took him back again and again? What drove him into the waters of baptism? What gave him strength in the ensuing years? My guess would be the message of hope the words gave him. As he said in those verses, he knew the hell that he had felt before, but now, he was willing to trust the completed work of Jesus, to trust all that the Lord said.

After retiring from the ministry at the age of seventy-six, Edward Mote said this: "I think I am going to heaven; yes, I am nearing port. The truths I have been preaching, I am now living upon and they'll do very well to die upon. Ah! The precious blood." [4]

From the time of his conversion to his final days, Edward Mote heard the song of hope as it filled his life with comfort and joy. On the other hand, Mark Barton had stopped his ears to that song and had reduced his life to hopelessness because of financial setbacks, depression, anxiety, and the inability to see beyond his own vision. How sad that billions more have died without that hope and that billions more are living today without that hope. They place their hopes in so much that eventually lets them down—money, talent, people, jobs, or any number of other things that are just that: things; the ephemeral, what is here today and may be gone tomorrow.

In my work as an instructional designer, I generally work as a contractor, not as a full-time employee. This means my fellow contractors and I generally don't get any paid time off, no vacation or paid holidays. Once, I was working for a company that took great care of their contractors, understanding the work done by each of us. One year, as Christmas approached, the management team called us

---

[4] Robert J. Morgan, "The Solid Rock," in *Then Sings My Soul,* (Nashville, TN: Thomas Nelson, 2003), Page 111.

in for a meeting in the afternoon. There was some speculation by the other IDs—new managers were coming in, the cubicles were being rearranged, things like that. I added my guess, my hope, that the company had decided to pay us all for Christmas Day and New Year's Day. At the meeting, it was announced that the company was engaging in some cost-cutting moves, and all contractors were being given a furlough for the week of Christmas and New Year's … without pay. Neither my hopes nor anyone else's panned out.

It's no fun to find out you're not going to be getting paid for a couple of weeks, especially during the Christmas season. Situations such as those are generally good breeding grounds for anxiety, resentment, and despair. But as I listened to the announcement and as the news sank in, I remembered a promise that was made a long time ago. "Be strong and of good courage, do not fear nor be afraid of them; for the Lord your God, He is the One who goes with you. He will not leave you nor forsake you" (Deuteronomy 31:6 NKJV).

Rahab put her confidence in that tiqvah, that cord of hope. She had heard the stories, which were over forty years old. Because of those stories, she believed in the power of the God who was watching the Israelites. Think of the courage it took to display that red cord in her window for all to see. It wasn't located on the inside window, where it might have been mistaken for a sign of the type of business being conducted in the house. It was hanging on the outside wall. It was there when the king and his men came back from their wild-goose chase; it was there all the days before the Israelites came and all during their march around the city. Rahab's hope was built on the promise of God. I can imagine she heard a song of hope in the shout of the Israelites on that final day and in the crumbling walls all around her house while her walls stood firm.

Even in our darkest pit, God is there. He has the rope to help us up. He'll give us a boost. Then, He'll be waiting when we reach the top to help us on the journey to that hoped-for "land that is brighter than day." As David said, "Our soul waits for the Lord; He is our help and our shield. For our heart shall rejoice in Him, because we have trusted in His holy name. Let Your mercy, O Lord, be upon us, just as we hope in You" (Psalm 33:20–22 NKJV).

John M. Henry said this: "Yesterday is experience. Tomorrow is hope. Today is getting from one to the other as best we can."

In my deepest sorrow, I can hear the song of hope as it rises in my heart, if I will take the time to listen. The song can calm my soul and help me rejoice, even in times of distress; it can allay my fears and help me rest in the darkest night.

The song can do the same for you. Hope can keep you going. Hope can get you through the roughest day or the longest night. Hope comforts when a loved one is lost. Hope strengthens when disease wracks the body. Hope says there's light at the end of the tunnel, and it's not a train; it's the glory of Jesus, sitting on the right hand of God.

— 12 —

The Promise of Hope

Hope's peace is in a newborn child, a gentle touch, a caring smile.

It's there when storms blow hard and wild, in the unseen sight of our next mile.

—"Hope Rises Up"

Lord, you know the hopes of the helpless. Surely you will hear their cries and comfort them.

—Psalm 10:17 (NLT)

I steer my bark with hope in the head, leaving fear astern. My hopes indeed sometimes fail, but not oftener than the forebodings of the gloomy.

—Thomas Jefferson

As I mentioned several chapters back, I've always been a big fan of the *Peanuts* comic strip. One of my favorites featured Linus and Lucy near the end of a series of strips that involved a rain that had lasted for several days. Lucy was looking out the window and finally wondered if the whole world would flood. Linus reassured her that, according to Genesis 9, God had promised the earth would never be completely flooded again and then sealed that promise with a rainbow. Lucy broke out in a smile and indicated she was reassured. In the last panel, Linus looked at her and said, "Sound theology has a way of doing that."

Yes, for those of us who are believers, sound theology can be most comforting and reassuring. But in this instance, it's more than just theology that's reassuring; it's the promise that God made to Noah and his descendants. "'Thus I establish My covenant with you: Never again shall all flesh be cut off by the waters of the flood; never again shall there be a flood to destroy the earth.' And God said: 'This is the sign of the covenant which I make between Me and you, and every living creature that is with you, for perpetual generations: I set My rainbow in the cloud, and it shall be for the sign of the covenant between Me and the earth'" (Genesis 9:11–13 NKJV).

That was and is a powerful promise and one that would put to rest not only the minds of Noah and his family but the minds of everyone to follow. Never again would they look at an extended rainfall and wonder, as Lucy did in the cartoon, "Is God flooding the earth again?" Every time a rainbow appeared, men and women and boys and girls could look at it and marvel not only at its beauty but at its meaning—the promise of God that the earth would not be destroyed again by water.

Promises

But just what is a promise?

According to the *Merriam-Webster* online dictionary, a promise is "a declaration that one will do or refrain from doing something specified; a legally binding declaration that gives the person to whom it is made a right to expect or to claim the performance or forbearance of a specified act." In essence, a promise says, "I'll do what I tell you I'm going to do, or I won't do what I tell you I won't do"—as in, "I'll never be late again. Honest!"

We'll make a lot of promises in our lifetimes. Some are rather lightweight—"I promise I'll call when I get there"; "I promise I'll never be late again"; "I promise to give you my undivided attention after the game is over." Some carry a great deal of weight—"I promise to tell the truth, the whole truth, and nothing but the truth"; "I promise I'll always be there for you." We make these promises with every intent of keeping them, but then, life gets in the way, our priorities change, and we lose our focus. We are, after all, only human.

But with God, a promise is a promise. "The Lord is not slack concerning His promise, as some count slackness, but is longsuffering toward us, not willing that any should perish but that all should come to repentance" (2 Peter 3:9 NKJV).

The promises of God are many and are important. I checked several sources and most agree that God makes over three thousand promises in the scriptures. Now, I'm pretty sure that I've made more promises than that in my lifetime, some of which I never intended to keep, I'm ashamed to say. You may have done the same at some time. But unlike you and me, God did not make promises lightly, and He does not take them lightly; they are His word, something upon which we can depend at all times.

Think about what I consider to be His first promise, found in Genesis 2:16–17: "And the Lord God commanded the man, saying, 'Of every tree of the garden you may freely eat; but of the tree of the knowledge of good and evil you shall not eat, for in the day that you eat of it you shall surely die'" (NKJV).

Now, some people may say, "That's a command, not a promise." True, but there's the promise of a consequence buried in there. After the first Gulf War, one of the conditions that General Norman Schwarzkopf put on the Iraqi military was that they could not use their air force. "You fly, you die," he promised. Here, God is telling Adam, "You try, you die!" In fact, Satan tried to convince Eve that it wasn't really a promise; it was just God wanting to be sure that humans stayed in their place. But Adam and Eve both learned the hard way that God's word is His bond, even if it means you have to die.

By the way, isn't it interesting that several centuries later, King Saul was put in a somewhat similar predicament? In 1 Samuel 14, we find the story of Saul rashly promising a curse on anyone who ate before vengeance was complete on his enemies, the Philistines. Unfortunately, his son, Jonathan, did not receive word of the fast. He was fainting from hunger, saw some honey, and took a small taste, which instantly refreshed him. The people soon followed his example, eating of the spoils of the Philistines. After some consultations, Saul relented of his oath, but the damage was done; God would not speak with him. So Saul made another rash promise: "Come over here, all you chiefs of the people, and know and see what this sin was today. For as the Lord lives, who saves Israel, though it be in Jonathan my son, he shall surely die." Lots were cast, and eventually, the lot fell on Jonathan. "I only tasted a little honey with the end of the rod that was in my hand. So now I must die!" Jonathan told Saul, who reluctantly agreed. But the people wouldn't hear of it because Jonathan had been instrumental in the defeat of the Philistines. Saul was swayed by their arguments and allowed his son to live. Imagine being a part of the nation of Israel at that time and seeing all this transpire. You would probably reach the conclusion that Saul's word was worthless, and his promises were empty.

God could not do that then, and He still cannot do that today. His promises are full of worth, words upon which we can rely, regardless of the circumstance. When Adam and Eve sinned, they had to suffer the promised consequence, despite the love God had for them. No, that's not right; they had to suffer the consequences *because of* the love He had for them. If He had not followed through, how could they—or any of us today—trust anything He said in scripture? "For I am the Lord, I do not change," God told us in Malachi 3:6.

As I mentioned, God made thousands more promises, both positive and negative. He promised Abraham a son, and Abraham got one. He promised the children of Israel that He'd take care of them. They were rescued from their slavery, crossed a dry seabed with waves towering over their heads, got water from a rock, received manna from heaven, and got quails to eat. God promised victories in battle, and they won those battles. He also promised that if Israel turned from Him, they'd pay the price. "But if you turn away and forsake My statutes and My commandments which I have set before you, and go and serve other gods, and worship them, then I will uproot them from My land which I have given them" (2 Chronicles 7:19–20 NKJV).

The people of Israel eventually learned the hard way that God keeps His promises.

The Importance of Promises

An important question to ask now is, "Why are promises so important?" The follow-up would be, "Why are God's promises so important?" The simple answer to both questions is that promises give us hope.

That hope is important with our everyday promises: I'll be on time, I'll do better, I'll have a surprise for you. Those promises can work to calm our hearts, to make us more willing to be patient and a little more understanding, especially when they're accompanied with a record of being kept.

But when we move from the secular to the spiritual world, promises take on a much deeper meaning and importance. God promised Abraham a son, and Paul tells us in Romans 4 that Abraham, in hope, believed, through his faith and contrary to what the world might say about his and Sarah's advanced age. Eventually, he became the father of many nations, according to what was spoken: "So shall your descendants be."

God, in His love for us, voluntarily made this promise to Abraham. The promise was part of another promise that He voluntarily made, again because of His love for us, right after Adam and Eve sinned. Addressing the serpent, God said, "And I will put enmity between you and the woman, and between your seed and her seed; He shall bruise your head, and you shall bruise His heel." This, of course, was the first allusion to His plan and promise to reconcile man to Him—His promise to send a Savior for all humankind. Prophecies of that promise are scattered throughout the Old Testament. Reference to it was made by Jesus Himself when He stood in the synagogue in Nazareth and read from Isaiah 61. Closing the book, He looked at those gathered in the assembly that day and said, "Today this scripture is fulfilled in your hearing."

Many that day were skeptical and would not believe. Some didn't care if He was who He said He was. It's the same today. But skepticism doesn't make the promise any less valid.

God's love made Him promise to give us a way back to Him; our faith in that promise and its fulfillment produces hope, the same type of hope that Noah, Leah, and Abraham had. It's the same with all the promises God makes in scripture. As David said, "Remember your promise to me; it is my only hope" (Psalm 119:49 NLT).

Because He made those promises, we have faith that He can see the arc of our lives. He understands the hurts and disappointments of the past; He sees the paths of hope laid out for the future. What we see as a wilderness is a vibrant forest in the Lord's footsteps; what we perceive as a wasteland is the seed of a new beginning with His mercy and grace.

What are the promises of hope God has made to you?

Comfort

Many years ago, I was asked by the head of the Sunday school at a congregation to teach the first graders. I really enjoyed the experience and learned a lot from those kids. However, the lesson series was a little strange; during one session I had to teach these six- and seven-year-olds about David and Bathsheba. Now that was a challenge! One of the other lessons was taken from John 14, which was the recounting of the time Jesus gave His final instructions to His apostles on the night before His crucifixion. I was using the King James Version at the time, and this is the way it reads: "And I will pray the Father, and He shall give you another Comforter, that He may abide with you forever; even the Spirit of truth; whom the world cannot receive, because it seeth Him not, neither knoweth Him: but ye know Him; for He dwelleth with you, and shall be in you" (John 14:16–17 KJV).

When Jesus spoke of the Comforter, He was, as we see in the next verse, referring to the Holy Spirit. I wanted to give the kids in the class some idea of who the Holy Spirit is and how He operates, though, to be honest, it's still difficult to understand fully, even for those of us Christians who've been looking at the subject for decades. Still, it was a class, and I had to instill something in those eager minds, so I fell back on the description Jesus gave. "What's a comforter?" I asked the class. I expected comments about their mothers comforting them in times of pain or about their dads putting arms around their shoulders after losing a soccer game. But one of the guys gave the most obvious answer of all: "It's that thing on my bed that keeps me warm." Now, that is a great definition of the Holy Spirit and the word of God. It's true that other translations use the words *Advocate*, *Helper*, and *Counselor*, but I really believe that in this verse, the King James Version gives a better sense of what Jesus was trying to say that night and what He'd been saying throughout the three years of His ministry. His words were not meant to condemn us. In fact, He specifically said that in John 3:17—"For God did not send His Son into the world to condemn the world, but that the world through Him might be saved." No, His words—and really, the words of the entire Bible—were meant to wrap us in a blanket of blessings and give us a warm hiding place from the cold reality of the world. His words were meant to give us hope. "For whatever things were written before were written for our learning, that we through the patience and comfort of the Scriptures might have hope" (Romans 15:4 NKJV).

Some people look at the Bible and see it as the words of a harsh, mean, and even genocidal god who doesn't want them to have any fun or a god who's given humans a list of things they can't do and the promise of fire and brimstone if they stray from those rules. Others look at it as a checklist that, if followed correctly and precisely, will allow them and the select few who do exactly as they do to get into heaven. But neither viewpoint is correct. The Bible is not a rule book; it's a guidebook. The words of God and the words of Jesus, contained in that collection of books and letters, written down by authors guided by the Comforter, are there to lead us to better and more fruitful lives, to strengthen us, and to comfort us, just as Paul said.

We all will go through trials and tribulations, heartache and despair, grief and loss. We're all going to wonder at some point if we can handle it any longer. In the midst of these trials, those of us who believe in this book can find in it a promise of comfort. The comfort may come from the words of a well-known passage, such as the Twenty-Third Psalm, or it may lie in the promise of something beyond the grief, the hope of rest in heaven. That's the type of comfort Paul discussed in 2 Corinthians 1:3–5: "Blessed be the God and Father of our Lord Jesus Christ, the

Father of mercies and God of all comfort, who comforts us in all our tribulation, that we may be able to comfort those who are in any trouble, with the comfort with which we ourselves are comforted by God. For as the sufferings of Christ abound in us, so our consolation also abounds through Christ" (NKJV).

I remember reading that when I was younger and thinking that it was pretty confusing. But the older I've gotten, the more I understand what Paul was saying, and the more comfort I've found in the words of Jesus and the promises of God. They have guided me to make many course corrections in my life and have helped me to learn that all is not lost, even in the worst of times. I've worked in places that have shut their doors, and I have been without a job for months. But because of the comfort I had in the Lord and the trust in His guidance, I was able to weather the storms and rest in the hope that things would work out for the best. They always did, though the outcome and the direction that I ended up traveling were much different than I anticipated.

That attitude spilled over into my secular life as well, which the Lord would certainly want to have happen. I'm sure most of you have discovered over the years that your attitude and reactions in times of stress and turmoil at your job or in other situations has made you the go-to "religious" person. "You're a religious guy; can you say grace at the meal?" But it's also made you the confidant of many a troubled person; you have become the friend who will listen and, if asked, pray for that person. We have been able to comfort others with the comfort we've found in Him, in His word, in His promises, and in the hope He offers.

When I think of this, I think of the great hymn writer Fanny Crosby. Blind from about six weeks of age, as she grew, she discovered a gift for words, writing her first poem at the age of eight. She ended up writing over eight thousand hymns and gospel songs; no doubt, one or two of them are your favorites. One of the most wonderful things about her hymns is that they are filled with images of seeing the works of God, seeing heaven, seeing Jesus, and seeing God. She didn't let her blindness become a crutch; she allowed God's rod and staff to guide her. She was able to see with a different vision, a heavenly vision.

Provision

In addition to comfort, God has promised to provide for our needs. One of the best passages demonstrating God's provision is found in Luke 12. Jesus is speaking to what we are told in the first verse is "an innumerable multitude of people." He begins by warning of the words of the hypocritical Pharisees; then He talks about the care and concern that God has for each of them. Someone asks Jesus to settle a financial dispute, at which point the Lord launches into a discourse about what's really important, beginning in verse 22:

> Then He said to His disciples, "Therefore I say to you, do not worry about your life, what you will eat; nor about the body, what you will put on. Life is more than food, and the body is more than clothing. Consider the ravens, for they neither sow nor reap, which have neither storehouse nor barn; and God feeds them. Of how much more value are you than the birds? And which of you by worrying can add one cubit to his stature? If you then are not able to do the least, why are you anxious for the rest? Consider the lilies, how they grow: they neither toil nor spin; and yet I say to you, even Solomon in all his glory was not arrayed like one of these. If then God so clothes the grass, which today is in the field and tomorrow is thrown into the oven, how much more will He clothe you, O you of little faith? And do not seek what you should eat or what you should drink, nor have an anxious mind. For all these things the nations of the world seek after, and your Father knows that you need these things. But seek the kingdom of God, and all these things shall be added to you." (Luke 12:22–31 NKJV)

It's rather striking what Jesus used for examples in this passage—ravens, height-challenged individuals (it makes one wonder if Zacchaeus was in the audience or at least heard about what Jesus said!), lilies, grass, and Solomon.

God had used ravens as an example for provision long before this parable. In Job 38:41, during his discourse to Job, God said, "Who provides food for the raven, when its young ones cry to God, and wander about for lack of food?" It's worth noting here that ravens are, for the most part, scavengers. Although they do eat some plants, berries, fruits, and grains, their main diet is carrion—you know, dead things. They scavenge on just about any type of dead meat; moose, goats, deer, cows, sheep, snakes, and rabbits are among their culinary delights. Back in Deuteronomy 14, ravens are on the list of unclean birds the Israelites were told not to eat; they were unclean, most likely because of their diet. Don't forget that in Numbers, God told the Israelites that any person who touched a dead body was considered unclean. Ravens and similar birds were, in a sense, perpetually unclean under that command. Yet God feeds them and provides for their dietary needs. It's all part of the great circle of life that Elton John sang about; the circle of life that God created.

Another type of provision Jesus speaks of here is clothing, which became more important after a certain couple noticed their nakedness in the garden of Eden. His example is the lilies of the field, which are beautiful flowers indeed. According to the *Encyclopedia Britannica*, because of their beauty, lilies have been used for ornamental purposes for thousands of years. If fact, Roman mythology tells us that Venus, goddess of beauty, was so jealous of the lily that she caused a large pistil to grow in the center of the bloom. In 1 Kings, we read that some of the decorations installed in the temple resembled lily blossoms. Those in His audience were well aware of the beauty of the lilies, so when He used that example, they could readily identify with it, just like the raven. All of that beauty is there for humans to enjoy, yet the lily does not have to harvest cotton or shear sheep to have the raw materials to clothe itself; the lily doesn't have to sit at a spinning wheel to pull together the raw materials. The lily puts no effort into its beauty; it simply grows in the way God designed it to grow. God prepares the soil, the nutrients, the rain, and the sunshine that the lily needs to become the beautiful flower so admired by many.

It's the same with grass. The word used here indicates more than just that stuff on your front lawn; it also means grains, such as wheat or hay. You may not think of either as beautiful, but a farmer or a landscaper would give you a good argument. Plus, think of the uses of both. Grass helps hold the soil in the land; hay is great feed for livestock; and wheat is a diet staple. The beauty isn't just in the outer covering; it's also in its functionality. While the wheat and the hay grow, you can see the beauty of the field every time the wind blows those "amber waves of grain" we sing about. Sometimes, the grass is literally thrown into the oven, yet God cares enough to clothe it with beauty while it lasts.

The people in the audience had never seen Solomon, nor had they seen the temple he built. But they had heard stories. They could see the second temple, and they had imaginations. "These plants are clothed by God with more beauty than Solomon with all his wealth could ever attain," Jesus tells them.

God's blessings to Solomon are a great example of His provision and grace. God said that He'd give Solomon anything, and Solomon asked for wisdom. God was so pleased with the choice that He gave Solomon wisdom and much more. His audience knew that, yet Jesus chose to make Solomon sort of an anti-example. "The lilies of the field are far more beautiful than Solomon in all his grandeur," is what the Lord is saying. God, who blessed Solomon with more than he'd asked for, takes care of the lilies and the grasses. Don't you think He cares about you? Don't you think He'll take care of you?

That's the $64,000 question, isn't it? We're just like those people in the audience, those people with little faith. It isn't easy to put everything in the hands of God, is it? We like to say we can do it, and we do, in some instances. But then, there are those times where we get a little edgy or those moments when we begin to wonder if He's really watching or listening—or hearing! It's in those times that we begin to lose focus, which is really what Jesus is talking about in this statement: "You focus on seeking to follow God, on seeking to serve Him; God will provide the rest."

Now, we've all heard that statement. "God provides" doesn't mean He gives us everything we want, but it means He gives us what we need. In fact, we've heard it so much it has become a cliché for many and gets glossed over a good bit. But just because it's a cliché doesn't mean it's not true. We've all been in some dark circumstances in our lives, times when we've lost jobs, suffered financial setbacks, or have seen our IRA or 401(k) sink. Sometimes, what we're going through is our own fault; sometimes, it's the fault of someone else; and sometimes, it's something completely out of anyone's control. It isn't easy to give it to God, but that's what He wants us to do, as a way of putting our faith into action.

Many years ago, we lived in a fourteen-by-seventy mobile home. Through a series of circumstances, we ended up with four adults and two babies living under that roof. We wanted out, as you can imagine, and had the financial resources to get a house, but the trick was that we had to sell the mobile home. I can tell you that I tried every way I could think and every kind of advertising imaginable. I even considered doing one of those raffle deals. Nothing was working. Finally, the light bulb went off. "Lord," I prayed, "we'd really like to be in a bigger house, but if this is where you want us, then so be it. We have a roof over our heads, and we thank you for that. We'll figure out a way to live here." The next week, out of the clear blue sky (yeah, right), a couple stopped by, took a quick tour, and told us they wanted to buy it. We were out of there within the next few months.

Now, your situation may be a lot worse than that, but the principle is the same. We have to do the best we can with what He gives us, focus on His kingdom, and let Him do the worrying for us. God promises to provide. If you don't believe me, just stop by a botanical garden and take a look at the lilies or just eat a piece of bread. If God feeds and clothes lilies and wheat, imagine what He can do for you. God provides, if we're willing to accept.

Fullness

The promise of provision leads to another promise—the promise of fullness.

Have you ever thought that God is a God of fullness? When the tabernacle was finished in Exodus 40, a cloud settled over the tent, and the glory of God filled the tabernacle. Notice it doesn't say, "He entered the tabernacle." The scripture says He filled it. In Deuteronomy 11, God promised to send grass in the fields for the livestock so the children of Israel could be filled. In 1 Kings 8, the glory of God, in the form of a cloud, fills the newly completed temple. God filled it so full that the priests couldn't do their tasks. Isaiah tells us in chapter 33 that God filled Zion with justice and righteousness.

Later, Jesus demonstrated the filling power of God. When Jesus turned water to wine in John 2, He told the men to fill the water pots, and they were filled to the brim. In Luke 5, Jesus told Simon and the others to launch out to the deep and cast their nets for a catch. The catch filled the nets and filled two boats with so many fish they began to sink.

God doesn't do things halfway.

The scriptures tell us about a couple of other interesting fillings involving Jesus. The fillings occurred when He fed the multitudes. In both instances, the people were able to eat their fill, and there was plenty left over. There were twelve baskets full one time and seven baskets the other. Jesus was concerned for their physical needs on both occasions, and He made sure they had sustenance for their bodies. He was also concerned for their other physical needs, healing many during one incident. But understand that Jesus was even more concerned with filling their spiritual needs. On both occasions, He took the time to fill their hearts and souls with His words and His guidance.

You can see this concern in two other quieter incidents.

In John 4, we read the story of Jesus speaking with a woman who was empty. She had not had an easy life. Later, we learn that she had been married five times and had probably grown so sour on the idea of marriage that she was now just living with a man. She was at a well in the middle of the day, under a blazing sun. She was struggling with a burden, her water pot. But that probably wasn't her only burden. She had no help from anyone. Was she angry? Ashamed? Bitter? We don't know, and Jesus never tells us. Instead, He addressed her as an equal, not worrying about her gender or her heritage. "Give Me a drink," He said. She was taken aback at the request, reminding Him of the ancient rivalry between Jews and Samaritans. But He pressed on with a cryptic message about living water, eventually telling her this: "Whoever drinks of this water will thirst again, but whoever drinks of the water that I shall give him will never thirst. But the water that I shall give him will become in him a fountain of water springing up into everlasting life" (John 4:13–14 NKJV).

The woman was filled with wonder at how well He knew her, and she was filled with curiosity. When He told her He was the Messiah, she immediately left.

Interestingly, it was at this point that the apostles returned from obtaining food. They urged Jesus to eat, but instead of filling His own body, He told them of the other spiritual filling of which He must partake. "I have food to eat of which you do not know," Jesus told them. "My food is to do the will of Him who sent Me, and to finish His work."

When the woman left the well and her water pot burden, she went back to town and told the townspeople about her encounter. "Could this be the Christ?" she asked them. Their interest was piqued too, and they all went back to Jesus. When they met Him, they urged Him to stay, and He did. Because of a woman who wanted to fill a water pot, many were filled with the words of Jesus. "Then they said to the woman, 'Now we believe, not because of what you said, for we ourselves have heard Him and we know that this is indeed the Christ, the Savior of the world'" (John 4:42 NKJV).

Another time Jesus mentions a filling is when He and the disciples were in Capernaum, on the day after the feeding of the five thousand with seven loaves and two fishes. "And Jesus said to them, 'I am the bread of life. He who comes to Me shall never hunger, and he who believes in Me shall never thirst'" (John 6:35 NKJV).

Many who heard these words in the sixth chapter had probably witnessed the miracle of the loaves and fishes. They had known physical hunger and thirst, and it had been satisfied. Now, He was telling them their spiritual hunger and thirst could be satisfied as well; they could be full of His word and the grace of God.

I can tell you right now that I'm always in need of this spiritual filling. The chances are pretty good that you are too, along with everyone else in the world. So many today are walking through this world wounded, lost, and hopeless. They can put up a good front and fool loved ones and friends, but they're never able to fool themselves.

When I was working on this chapter, the news came out about a young lady in New York who had taken her own life. She was just twenty-seven years old. She had a good job and had what seemed a good life. But the following is part of what she wrote in her suicide note:

> I have accepted hope is nothing more than delayed disappointment, and I am just plain old-fashioned tired of feeling tired. I realize I am undeserving of thinking this way because I truly have a great life on paper. I'm fortunate to eat meals most only imagine. I often travel freely without restriction. I live alone in the second greatest American city (San Francisco, you'll always have my heart). However, all these facets seem trivial to me. It's the ultimate first world problem, I get it. I often felt detached while in a room full of my favorite people; I also felt absolutely nothing during what should have been the happiest and darkest times in my life. No single conversation or situation has led me to make this decision, so at what point do you metaphorically pull the trigger? [5]

The article stated she was from San Francisco, so her family was a continent away, but I'm sure she had friends, companions, coworkers, and acquaintances. Yet there was that one telling statement midway through the note: "I live alone." She had what many would consider a full life, yet she was empty. I'd hazard a guess and say that her life wasn't quite as full as she or any of her friends thought. She was missing something in her heart and something in her soul. She was missing the love of God, the love of Christ, and the touch of the Holy Spirit. I used

---

[5] Tina Moore, Natalie Musumeci, "Young Manhattan dietician Tara Condell hanged herself after posting suicide note," from the *New York Post* website, January 1, 2019

this a few chapters back, but it bears repeating here: "That Christ may dwell in your hearts through faith; that you, being rooted and grounded in love, may be able to comprehend with all the saints what is the width and length and depth and height—to know the love of Christ which passes knowledge; that you may be filled with all the fullness of God" (Ephesians 3:17–19 NKJV).

People don't realize how spiritual the Three Stooges can be, if you look beyond the silliness. In one film, they are so poor that they don't have money for food. So they eat imaginary soup, even blowing on it to cool it so it won't burn their tongues. But when the imaginary meal is done, they are still empty.

This young lady was feasting on an empty life and hearing empty words and empty promises, just as we all do sometimes. Even Christians, from time to time, think that something's missing. We can be full of His love, full of His grace, and full of the knowledge of Him. But it does take effort on our part. Earlier, I quoted John 6:35. Jesus said, "I am the bread of life. He who comes to Me shall never hunger, and he who believes in Me shall never thirst" (NKJV). We have to go to Him, and we have to believe. When we move toward Jesus, move in God's direction, follow the Holy Spirit, and patiently endure, we get closer to the promise of being filled with Him. We get closer to the promise of being a part of His family.

A Home

I have a photo of my brother and me taken in the early '60s. He was a suave teenager; I was a geeky kid. We both wore sharp-looking suits, though, and I had a cool bow tie. We were standing in front of my dad's '55 Chevy, which sat in our carport. I've always liked that photograph, but once as I was looking at it, I began to see more in the photo. I started noticing the carport and remembering how my dad would pull the car out on Saturdays during the summer and fire up the charcoal grill on that concrete pad. I thought of the back porch just behind the carport, where we would sit and turn the hand crank of the ice-cream maker. Looking at the photo, I could see the clothesline out back and remember clothes flapping in the breeze after my mom washed them. Thinking of the backyard led me to the Wiffle ball games and croquet matches my dad, brother, sister, and I played (my mom wasn't into those games, but she would watch). Finally, I recalled those summer nights when we sat in lawn chairs in the backyard at night, talking and catching fireflies—being a family.

I've been back to that house a few times. It sure does look small now. But the home my parents made inside that house was huge, and that home still touches the lives of their grandchildren and great-grandchildren today.

The Lord has promised us a home as well—two, to be precise.

The first is the church. Many in the world think of the church as just a building, as a place where people go to fulfill their obligation to attend, well, church. But we know better; we know it is our home here on earth. That house on Tilson Road in Decatur, Georgia, where I spent so many years was a nice place to live, but it was the people in the family who lived there that gave it life and made it a home. It is the people who inhabit the Lord's church who give it life as well and who make it a home. We are brothers and sisters in Christ and are part of the same family. We have a shared blood heritage—the blood of Jesus.

The church is us, and because it's us, we should learn how to make each other feel loved and cared for, warm and comfortable. All through Paul's letters, he encourages Christians to build each other up, to comfort each other, to edify each other, and to guard each other. The church is there not just as a body to worship God but as a body to strengthen each other. It is there to welcome others into the family. As the called-out of God, we should strive to make the church in general and our local congregation specifically into the type of home in which any visitor would feel welcome and would enjoy spending time.

But that's only the beginning because we have the promise of another home: "Then the King will say to those on His right hand, 'Come, you blessed of My Father, inherit the kingdom prepared for you from the foundation of the world'" (Matthew 25:34 NKJV).

That's the home we're all waiting for—heaven. This is the ultimate promise. Lots of people have speculated about what heaven will be like.

In Revelation, the apostle John tried to describe it for us, but it was just beyond words.

When I've had a hard day, I enjoy getting home and resting in the comfort of my home. When I've had a hard week, I enjoy starting the next one, resting in the comfort of my spiritual family, the church. When this life is over, I look forward to resting in the comfort of the arms of the Savior and in the peace that awaits in heaven.

Linus said to Lucy that sound theology has a way of making us feel better. But that's not really true; it's the promises of God that really do it. And isn't it wonderful to know that we have those promises, made by someone who keeps all His promises?

We have the promise of comfort in times of trouble, pain, and sorrow.

We have the promise of provision; though it might not be what we want, it's what we need.

We have the promise of fullness, not just physical but spiritual, hearts full of the love, mercy, and guidance of God, Jesus, and the Holy Spirit.

We have the promise of a home here on this earth; the promise of a safe place for us to gather strength from like-minded lovers of the Lord.

Finally, we have the promise of a home beyond this one, with a brand-new mansion waiting for us. It will be a home where there is no night because it is filled with the glory of God.

Those are the promises we can build our hope upon and the promises we can count on.

Afterword

And in the End

Then when we reach the journey's end,
Hope reaches out and folds us in and introduces our best friend,
The One who's been beside us all the while.
There's nothing like the hope in Jesus's smile.
—"Hope Rises Up"

When the Chief Shepherd appears, you will receive
the crown of glory that does not fade away.
—1 Peter 5:4 (NKJV)

Here bring your wounded hearts, here tell your anguish;
Earth has no sorrow that Heaven cannot heal.
—Thomas More

This is the way I think it'll be:

My eyes will close for the last time. What pain there may have been will quickly dissipate as I hear a faint rustling sound. I'll open my eyes again to see angels standing around me.

"It's all right," one will say with a big smile. "We're here to guide you."

Slowly, quietly, we'll go away from that place, from this place. The memories of the hospital, of jobs and time schedules, of money and all things earthly will vanish. They'll never be with me again. We'll move on toward a brilliant light, brighter than any sun imagined. I won't be blinded by the radiance; I'll need no sunglasses. The warmth will fill my soul.

They'll take me to a mansion more splendid and finer than any house I ever had or could ever have wanted on earth. They'll give me a tour, then hand me the deed. Next, I'll get the guided tour of heaven as they take me on toward the center of the light. In the distance, I'll hear singing—"Hallelujah, Praise Jehovah"; "Sing the Wondrous Love of Jesus"; "Victory in Jesus"; "Holy, Holy, Holy"—sung as never before, with voices that sound sweeter than the sweetest bird on a bright spring morning. As we near the center, the singing will become louder and even more joyous. There, I'll see millions upon millions gathered around a throne. On the throne will be the light.

Other angels will be guiding others like me. We'll smile at each other and embrace. "Congratulations." "What a wonderful place." "Peace of God."

Peace of God. Perfect peace.

Someone will approach. He'll smile at me and hug me tightly, more tightly than anyone ever has before. "Welcome, son. I hope you like the mansion I built for you." Then a nail-scarred hand will take mine. "Come with me," He'll say.

We'll walk through the millions who are gathered around the throne. And somewhere, we'll stop. My elder brother will reach down and tap someone on the shoulder. "There are some people who'd like to see you," He'll say.

They'll slowly stand and turn. When they see me, their eyes will widen with joy.

"Scott, it's you!" they'll shout and throw their arms around me. "We're so glad you're here again."

"Yeah, it's me, Mama and Daddy," I'll answer, hugging them back.

They'll clasp me by the shoulders and take a long look at me. "Welcome home," they'll say.

There will be no tears—no tears of joy or sadness. We'll sit and talk of the Father and the Son and the Holy Spirit. We'll sing. We'll enjoy each other's company once again. It'll be like those days in the backyard, only better—much better.

I won't apologize for not telling them how much I loved them and appreciated them. They knew it all along anyway. We won't talk of those who are still left behind because that would bring tears, and the Father won't allow that to happen.

On their faces there will be no wrinkles, and no scars will mar their appearance. They will be the faces I remember, but somehow different. Their eyes will dance with the joy of being in the presence of the Father. In those eyes, in those faces, I'll see only one thing: glory.

You see, because of the love of God and Jesus and because of the gift of the Holy Spirit, I can look past this life. I can see the light at the end of the tunnel.

The light in the tunnel isn't a train. It's the glory of the Father.

It's my hope.

My hope of glory.

All This and Heaven Too

I have been baptized in the cleansing flood; all my sins washed away by the Savior's blood.

Now my soul is clean, and my heart is clear. He has taken the doubt; He has taken the fear.

I have joy; I have peace; I have found release. He gives hope that will carry me through.

In my time of need, I've a friend indeed. I have all this and heaven too.

All this and heaven too.

As I walk along in the shadow of sin and temptations that threaten to pull me in,

There's a light I can follow, if I only will; leads me safe through the valley and on to the hill.

I have courage to stand when I don't think I can. He gives strength that will carry me through.

When the world is cold, I've a hand to hold; I have all this and heaven too.

All this and heaven too.

And when time has flown till my body fails, He'll send angels to guide me on my last trail.

He will welcome me to the home He's prepared, free at last from all sorrows, worries, and cares.

All my family and friends I will see once again, and then some faces that I never knew.

He'll say, "They were hopeless and alone, but you helped lead them back home,

So they'd have all that and heaven too—all that and heaven too.

Acknowledgments

This book took a long time to write. I first had the idea in the mid-1990s and played around with it in fits and starts. People read sample chapters from time to time, but it wasn't until a few years ago that I finally decided it was time.

When Alan Jackson first won a country music award, he gave a long acceptance speech because he had lots of people to thank and didn't know if he'd ever get up there again. I know how he felt.

Special thanks to my editors: Karyn Fogel, Judy Parker, Linda Vaughn, Tim Weekley, and Steve Zimpfer. You found lots of little things (and big things) that I was able to correct to make these words sound better. Thank you for giving of your time so willingly to make this happen.

Thanks to the fine folks at iUniverse for helping me make this dream come true.

Thanks to the men and women who have made a huge impact on my spiritual walk and whose sermons and teachings inspired me: W. D. McPherson, Thelma McPherson, Horace Walton, Joyce Green, Ted Garner, Ronnie Bush, Jody Vickery, Jean Robert St. Hilaire, David Decker, Harold Savage, Brian Whelchel, and so many more.

Thanks to Cathy Wiley, who told me not to lose my salt.

Thanks to the teachers who made a huge difference in my writing: Rita Campbell, Frances Abercrombie, Dawn Pitts, Elsie Smith, Mrs. Arnett (I'm sorry; I never knew your first name), and Dixie Lee Ray. You taught and inspired me. Thanks to my former boss, Vee Nelson, who helped me become a better writer.

Thanks to my dad, Ralph White, who was a spiritual giant and a great father. Thanks to my mom, Angie White, who was always there to listen to me, encourage me, and support me. Thanks to my brother, Ray, and my sister, Charlotte, who've had a bigger impact on me than they'll ever know—and have finally stopped picking on me!

Thanks to my wife, Angie, who puts up with me for some reason. I love you, Angel! Thanks to all my children and grandchildren who've taught me a little bit about patience (which I'm still trying to perfect) and who help make my life complete.

Finally, thanks, especially and always, to God, Jesus, and the Spirit. You saved my soul, gave me this gift, and continue to guide me, even when I don't think I need guidance. I am filled with Your promises, and I hope for Your glory every day.